Critical Thinking and Education

Issues and Ideas in Education Series
edited by Robin Barrow, School of Education,
University of Leicester

Dilemmas of the Curriculum
G. H. BANTOCK

Happiness
ROBIN BARROW

John Stuart Mill's Theory of Education
F. W. GARFORTH

Educational Practice and Sociology
B. SHAW

Behaviorism and Schooling
IRA S. STEINBERG

Liberty in Education
KENNETH STRIKE

Fantasy and Common Sense in Education
JOHN WILSON

Critical Thinking and Education

JOHN E. McPECK

The University of
Western Ontario

MARTIN ROBERTSON · OXFORD

For Jeanne, Heather and Jenny

First published in 1981 by
Martin Robertson & Company Ltd.,
108 Cowley Road, Oxford OX4 1JF.

British Library Cataloguing in Publication Data

McPeck, John E.
   Critical Thinking and Education. - (Issues and
   ideas in education)
   1. Cognition
   I. Title II. Series
   153.4'2   BF311

   ISBN 0-85520-383-8
   ISBN 0-85520-384-6 (Pbk)

Typeset in 11 on 12 point Andover by
Photosetting & Secretarial Services Limited, Yeovil.
Printed and bound in Great Britain by Book Plan, Worcester.

Contents

Acknowledgements

Since this book was written on a small island where library facilities were limited, it owes much more to communication with other people than might normally be the case. I would, therefore, like to thank them. There is first Robin Barrow, who went beyond the duties of a normal editor, and whose guidance, support and constant encouragement literally made this book possible. Special thanks are also due to my colleague and friend, James T. Sanders, who is never bothered by my chaotic prose, and who always seemed to grasp my ideas more clearly than myself. My wife, Jeanne, not only typed and proofed the original manuscript from a defective typewriter, but her quiet patience also helped expose many defective arguments. The constant supply of contraband paper from my colleague, Geoff Milburn, had its intended effect. Shirley Skinner did a fine job, as usual, typing the final draft. And to all those who mailed things from far-off places, thank you.

For permission to quote extensively from copyright material, I gratefully acknowledge the following:

McGraw-Hill Book Company for selected material from *Reasoning* by Michael Scriven (1976); *Harvard Educational Review* for selected material from 'A Concept of Critical Thinking' vol. 32, no. 1 (Winter 1962), by Robert Ennis; Edgepress for selected material from *Informal Logic: The First International Symposium*, edited by R. H. Johnson and J. A. Blair (1980); Harcourt Brace Jovanovich for selected passages from the *Watson–Glazer Critical Thinking Appraisal* and the accompanying *Manual* (1964); Maurice Temple Smith Co. for permission to quote material from *Teaching Thinking* by Edward de Bono (1976). I would also like to thank the American Philosophy of Education Society for allowing me to reprint a portion of chapter 2 that appears in their 1981 *Proceedings* under the title 'Critical thinking without logic: restoring dignity to information', written by myself.

John E. McPeck
London, Ontario

CHAPTER 1

The Meaning of Critical Thinking

Among people who bother to think about education at all, reflective parents, theorists, radical reformers and traditionalists alike, there is a prevailing opinion that the ability to think critically is a desirable human trait, and that for this reason it should be taught in our schools whenever possible. Being in favour of critical thinking in our schools is thus a bit like favouring freedom, justice or a clean environment: it meets with general approval from the outset. But as with those other concepts, it is not at all clear that people mean the same thing by critical thinking, nor that they would all continue to approve of it if they did agree about what it meant. For very often with such matters approval diminishes in inverse proportion to the clarity with which they are perceived. One might, in fact, take such wide and diverse approval of critical thinking as an index of the vagueness of the concept. On the assumption that enlightened disagreement is preferable to consensus formed in the dark, I shall attempt to clarify the concept of critical thinking and to draw out its curriculum implications. If this can be done, agreement and disagreement on the issue will at least be intelligible.

The problem has not been a dearth of literature on critical thinking; on the contrary, journal discussions and pre-packaged curricula are legion. The problem is that there is no precise way of assessing this material in the absence of an understanding of what the concept entails and what it precludes. At the moment, the persistent vagueness of the concept supports curriculum proposals ranging from courses in Latin to logic and clever puzzle games. All such proposals have claimed to promote critical thinking.

In addition to the vagueness of the concept, there are several closely related questions that require separate elucidation. For example, clarifying what critical thinking is may not guarantee an answer to the question of whether it is teachable, let alone how to teach it. And even if we had answers to these questions, the nature of the connection between critical thinking and education requires more precise consideration than it has enjoyed heretofore. What is clear, however, is that at the centre of this cluster of issues is the question of what critical thinking *is*. Without an answer to this question one cannot begin to answer any of the others. Let us clear the ground first.

What critical thinking is not

On the surface at least, it would appear that the phrase 'critical thinking' simply refers to the careful and precise thinking that is used to resolve some problem. Indeed, this is perhaps not far from the truth. But what, we might ask, is responsible for all the confusion and contradictory proposals surrounding this rather straightforward idea?

The confusion stems from approaching the concept as though it were a self-evident slogan whose precise ingredients were considered to be clear and self-justifying by those who favour its promulgation. The phrase 'critical thinking' is both over-worked and under-analysed in the same way that the term 'education' was before the work of R. S. Peters. Even the more careful work that has been done on critical thinking tends to rush over the analysis of the basic concept and to move on to itemizing the various skills that it is thought to involve. For example, Robert Ennis's landmark paper 'A concept of critical thinking'[1] simply declares that critical thinking means 'the correct assessment of statements'. But nowhere does he provide a justification for this view. Furthermore, it is quite clear that this is *not* what critical thinking means, since one could correctly assess a statement without having done so critically (one could do it by chance, for instance). In addition, there are many activities (for example, mountain climbing) and skills (chess, competitive wrestling and so on) that permit critical thought but do not necessarily involve the 'assessment of statements'. My point here is not so much that Ennis's view is mistaken, but rather that his mode of procedure is typical in giving short shrift to the conceptual analysis of what is being discussed, that is, critical thinking.

Whatever critical thinking may be precisely, it is quite clear that it is *thinking* of some sort. Perhaps for this reason, research in this area has been dominated by psychologists.[2] However, such research is unfortunately characterized by studies of very specific types of thinking, such as inductive or deductive reasoning or specific types of problem solving, as in chess, spatial reasoning, calculating and so forth. It has not therefore provided a conceptual analysis of critical thinking in general. We need to ask what, if anything, all the instances have in common.

Thinking sometimes just happens to us, as in daydreams, passing impressions or even hallucinations (that is, involuntarily), and at other times it is intentional and directed (voluntary). A case might be made to the effect that dreams and other forms of involuntary thinking sometimes help us solve problems, but this is not the type of thinking of concern here, since it is not the kind that can be directly taught, and in any case it would not qualify for the adjective 'critical'.[3] It is important to note, however, that thinking is always thinking *about* something. To think about nothing is a conceptual impossibility. The importance of this simple point is that it raises serious questions about the meaning of such commonly heard claims as 'I teach thinking', or 'I teach students to think.' One may well ask 'About what?' Nor would the claim that one taught 'thinking in general' or 'thinking about everything' be any more helpful. For to think about nothing in particular is equivalent to not thinking at all. And to think of 'everything in general' is incoherent. On the other hand, if the claim 'I teach students to think' is intended to mean 'Every time some particular thing occurs to a student, I teach him to think about it', then it must mean one of two things. It is either the vacuous tautology 'Every time a student thinks about something I teach him to think about *that* something', or it means 'Every time he thinks about something I teach him to think *more* about that something.' This latter claim is meaningful, but it is important to realize that what constitutes 'thinking more about something', apart from holding the identical thought in the mind longer, must be adding something to it, making finer discriminations with respect to it or otherwise changing one's perspective of it. In each case of thinking about something or thinking *more* about something there is a singling out, or particularization, from an infinite plethora of other possible thoughts. In other words, it is a matter of conceptual truth that thinking is always *thinking about* X, and that X can never be 'everything in general' but must always be something in particular. Thus the claim 'I teach students to think' is at worst false and at best misleading.

Thinking, then, is logically connected to an X. Since this fundamental point is reasonably easy to grasp, it is surprising that critical thinking should have become reified into a curriculum subject and the teaching of it an area of expertise of its own. One of the reasons for this is perhaps a new and progressive emphasis on the *critical* part of critical thinking. It might seem that if one focuses on the adjective 'critical', the particular object of thought becomes relatively unimportant or incidental. But this view ignores the fact that the adjective 'critical' simply qualifies 'thinking' (both grammatically and in fact), and so critical thinking, too, must be directed toward something.

The adjective 'critical' describes a kind of thinking, just as do 'precocious', 'imaginative', 'creative', 'sensitive' and so on. But they do not describe what is being thought about. Thus when one drops the X, or merely the emphasis on X, from the sentence 'I teach critical thinking about X', one arrives at a statement that is equivalent to 'I teach imagin- ation', 'I teach precocity', 'I teach creativity'. And even if some sense can be made of the claim that creativity, imagination and critical thinking are general skills, it can be seen that they must be the concomitants of other pursuits, since they are related to the way in which something is done, not what is done (for example, 'She plays the piano *sensitively*'). Adding the adjective 'critical' to the phrase 'thinking about X' describes in some general way *how* something is thought about, but it does not describe that something. In isolation from a particular subject, the phrase 'critical thinking' neither refers to nor denotes any particular skill. It follows from this that it makes no sense to talk about critical thinking as a distinct subject and that it therefore cannot profitably be taught as such. To the extent that critical thinking is not about a specific subject X, it is both conceptually and practically empty. The statement 'I teach critical thinking', *simpliciter*, is vacuous because there is no generalized skill properly called critical thinking.

What is critical thinking?

What is it, then, that we are trying to convey and, more important, to achieve when we talk about getting people to think critically? We can, after all, use the phrase 'critical thinking' in perfectly meaningful ways. Moreover, its meaning is distinguishable from the meanings of 'imaginative thinking', 'sensitive thinking', 'creative thinking' and the like. It has already been argued that thinking is always thinking about something – for example, some problem, activity or subject area. And only such things as problems, activities or subjects can be thought about critically. Critical thinking always manifests itself in connection with some identifiable activity or subject area and never in isolation. Consequently, just as there are innumerable activities and types of activity that can be thought about critically, so there are innumerable ways in which critical thinking can be manifested. Just as certain activities can be done well or poorly, so certain activities can be done critically or uncritically. There are many distinct types of behaviour that could count as 'critical thinking behaviour'. In some instances, such behaviour might outwardly manifest itself in an act requiring physical strength, in others dexterity, perhaps most often in the assessment of statements of some kind.

Given the large spectrum of activities that allow of critical thinking, there is likely to be a correspondingly large number of criteria for the correct application of the phrase. In this sense the phrase 'critical thinking' functions like the term 'creative': actions that deserve the epithet vary widely, but the intended meaning is constantly identifiable.[4] Just as scientists, engineers, lecturers and artists can all display creative thought, so can they all display critical thought. Indeed, in many instances the final product of each kind of thinking might be indistinguishable to the observer, but this does not render their meanings identical. Usually, if one says that something is 'creative', one means to imply that it is novel and/or aesthetically appealing. If one describes a certain thought or bit of thinking as 'critical', however, one does not require it to be novel or aesthetically appealing. A 'critical' thought might issue in something novel or appealing, but it does not necessarily do so.

On the surface at least, perhaps the most notable characteristic of critical thought is that it involves a certain scepticism, or suspension of assent, towards a given statement, established norm or mode of doing things. This scepticism might ultimately give way to acceptance, but it does not take truth for granted. Instead, it considers alternative hypotheses and possibilities. Such thought might result in the detection of a fallacy, but it might equally well prompt a decision not to apply a perfectly well established rule, principle or procedure in a given instance. Indeed, the solution of many difficult problems often requires just that. In part, critical thinking involves seeing when a certain common procedure is fruitless by entertaining alternatives to it.

However, this scepticism is not pervasive or unjustified; that is, it is not automatically applied to every statement, argument or mode of doing things that one encounters. As John Passmore has pointed out:

> We can imagine someone who was so drilled that to any assertion he responded with 'I question that!', however

inappropriate the response in relation to its association. Such a person might be said to have formed a habit of questioning, but he would certainly not have learned to be critical.[5]

Rather, critical thinking requires the judicious use of scepticism, tempered by experience, such that it is productive of a more satisfactory solution to, or insight into, the problem at hand. At least, this is why it is invoked. It is important to realize that the criterion for regarding scepticism as judicious, as opposed to incorrect or frivolous, must be determined by the norms and standards of the subject area in question. Learning to think critically is in large measure learning to know when to question something, and what sorts of questions to ask. Not just any question will do.[6]

In short, critical thinking does not consist in merely raising questions, as many questions are straightforward requests for information. Nor does it involve indiscriminate scepticism, for that would ultimately be self-defeating, since it leads to an infinite regress. Rather, it is the appropriate use of *reflective scepticism* within the problem area under consideration. And knowing how and when to apply this reflective scepticism effectively requires, among other things, knowing something about the field in question. Thus we may say of someone that he is a critical thinker about X if he has the propensity and skill to engage in X (be it mathematics, politics or mountain climbing) with reflective scepticism. There is, moreover, no reason to believe that a person who thinks critically in one area will be able to do so in another. The transfer of training skills cannot be assumed of critical thinking but must be established in each case by empirical tests. Calling to witness such notorious cases as distinguished logicians with no idea for whom to vote, nor why, it is fair to postulate that no one can think critically about everything, as there are no Renaissance men in this age of specialized knowledge.

Since critical thinking is always 'critical thinking about X', it follows that critical thinking is intimately connected with other fields of knowledge. Thus the criteria for the judicious use of scepticism are supplied by the norms and standards of the field under consideration. Surprisingly, this simple insight runs against the general trend of textbooks on the subject, written primarily by philosophers, which stress certain logical skills. Every text that I have seen on critical thinking emphasizes some procedure for the detection of fallacies by using either formal or informal logic. This is due in no small part, I think, to what I call 'the philospher's fallacy'. This fallacy consists in regarding a *necessary* condition of critical thinking, namely a concern for logic, as a *sufficient* condition for critical thinking. I am not suggesting that logic has nothing to do with critical thinking, but rather that it plays a comparatively minor role – particularly when compared with knowledge of, and experience in, a specific field. Logic texts and critical thinking courses tend to play down this very important point by analysing readily accessible newspaper editorials and advertisements as though this exercise alone were sufficient to create a critical thinker. But logicians and philosophers have no monopoly on the use of logic; at most, they have a monopoly on the specific study of logic. No scientist, historian or archaeologist worth his salt is ignorant of the importance of avoiding contradictions, but consistency in itself is a long way from being sufficient to make him a critical thinker in his field. Knowledge of some natural language, like logic, is often a necessary condition for engaging in many activities, but it is seldom a sufficient condition. It is noteworthy that Robert Ennis's analysis of the concept of critical thinking points out that critical thinking has three dimensions: a logical dimension, a criterial dimension and a pragmatic dimension.[7] The last two dimensions have nothing to do with the detection of fallacies, or with logic as such, but have to do with specific knowledge of a subject area. It is therefore all the more surprising, though typical, that much of his analysis should focus on 'definition', 'ambiguity' and other topics from elementary logic.

I have already suggested that the core meaning of critical thinking is the propensity and skill to engage in an activity with reflective scepticism. However, this definition leaves room for ambiguities, which I would like to clarify. First, since it involves the skills necessary for engaging in an activity, critical thinking cannot be divorced from the skills that make the activity what it is. For example, critical thinking about an historical question requires, first and foremost, the skills of an historian; similarly, critical thinking about a scientific question requires the knowledge and skills of a scientist. There is no set of supervening skills that can replace basic knowledge of the field in question. Secondly, the phrase 'reflective scepticism', like 'healthy scepticism', refers to both the purpose and the quality of the thinking in question. The purpose of this scepticism is not to be disagreeable, but to advance progress toward the resolution of a problem. And we refer to it as 'reflective' if it demonstrates a quality or level of deliberation that at least appears to be capable of offering a plausible alternative. The concept of critical thinking might also be expressed more formally, if we prefer, as follows:

Let X stand for any problem or activity requiring some mental effort.

Let E stand for the available evidence from the pertinent field or problem area.

Let P stand for some proposition or action within X.

Then we can say of a given student (S) that he is a critical thinker in area X if S has the disposition and skill to do X in such a way that E, or some subset of E, is suspended as being sufficient to establish the truth or viability of P.

Notice that this analysis of critical thinking does not guarantee that success will issue from its employment: it, like education, is a 'task' and 'achievement' concept. The sceptical suspension of E might, in fact, lead to further confusion, in which case it would simply not be effective; it is undertaken, however, with the intention, or hope, of producing a better resolution to a problem. It is therefore no contradiction to say of S, 'S is a critical thinker in X but is not particularly good at it', because skills admit of degrees. Skills in general, we might note, are born of knowledge of, and experience in, specific areas. Merely meeting the logical requirements of consistency and so on would not be sufficient to characterize someone as skilful (unless the skill were doing logic as such): thus skills, like critical thinking in general, are parasitic upon detailed knowledge of, and experience in, parent fields and problem areas. The lion's share of E (above) comes from these areas. Moreover, critical thinking may be detrimental to the learning of many activities (for example, reading). Again, however, judgements about when its use is appropriate are best made by specialists in the field in question. Logicians can only check that certain necessary conditions are being met, but that task has no bearing on the question of whether people are ready to recognize them.

One of the more important implications of this analysis of critical thinking is that its scope is sufficiently broad to include processes involved in general problem solving, as well as some of the mental processes underlying more specific performances and skills, such as chess playing, mountain climbing, acting, theatre directing and many other activities requiring conscious mental effort. It is not restricted to the 'assessment of statements' (as Ennis claims),[8] nor to the detection of fallacies (as logic texts claim), but includes many other valid educational activities that do not necessarily have the pursuit of truth as their primary *raison d'être*. For example, in the areas of art, music, drama and perhaps mathematics we are likely to be concerned less with the truth of something than with the techniques involved in its execution (including such things as methods and strategies, the judicious use, and perhaps modification, of which lend themselves to critical thinking). While it is true that we can often reconstruct methods and strategies as propositions or statements *ex post facto*, it would be rash to think that critical thinking is restricted to the assessment of these propositions and statements. Doing things like solving problems and using methods often requires as much critical acumen as assessing statements within or about these activities.[9] Decisions about whether to employ this strategy rather than that, to modify a method in a certain way or even to disregard or change some standard technique are all grist to the critical thinker's mill, and it is grist that neither formal nor informal logic can grind, since logic is restricted to propositions. Indeed, it might be argued that most educational activities are preoccupied less with the assessment of statements or even the pursuit of truth than with inculcating in students certain intellectual skills, methods and modes of thinking. It is clear, for example, that Jerome Bruner's prescription for teaching the 'structure of disciplines' is attempting to do this, and it is also inherent in what I understand by R. S. Peters's notion of 'education as initiation' into certain worthwhile 'forms of thought'. And recent trends in moral education emphasize not the assessment of statements, nor what to think, but methods of resolving moral problems. All these proposals attempt to teach disciplined thinking of one kind or another. A disciplined mind is not incompatible with a critical mind; on the contrary, criticism without discipline is frivolity.

This analysis of critical thinking, which includes the active engagement in activities as well as the assessment of statements, obviously contains some of what Gilbert Ryle referred to as 'knowing how' as distinct from knowing that'; that is, it includes the use of skills. However, the types of skill to which I am drawing attention are those that have identifiable intellectual components, such as the use or partial use of various methods (research methods, statistical methods, programming methods), strategies (for solving problems, winning battles or games, attacking mountains) and techniques (crystallography *versus* spectrometry, models *versus* pictures, telling *versus* showing). The distinctions between these are not airtight, of course; it is clear that they involve more than 'knowing that', yet they are not pure and simple skills like balancing a bicycle or singing a high C, of the ingredients of which the possessor might not be consciously aware.[10] Not all skills permit the use of critical thinking, but a considerable number do. Furthermore, these are typically the very sorts of skill that educators are concerned to teach.

Michael Polanyi, in his lucid discussion of skills, defines a skill as 'the observance of a set of rules which are *not* known as such to the person following them'; and he uses swimming and bicycle riding as paradigm cases of skills.[11]

But this view of skills is restrictive because it cannot account for such things as methods, strategies and techniques, the rules of which are 'known as such to the person following them'. Moreover, it is not clear that the sort of 'observance of rules' that Polanyi has in mind requires any thinking whatever (let alone critical thinking), therefore the sense in which one can be said to be 'observing a rule' is not clear. While it is possible – indeed, common – for a person to engage in an activity (for example, scientific research) in which he employs certain methods and procedures routinely, this is not to say that he cannot scrutinize these procedures or recognize their deficiencies while using them. Indeed, such scrutiny represents one of the highest forms of critical thinking.

While critical thinking is perfectly compatible with rationality, and with reasoning generally, we should not regard the terms as equivalent. The concept of critical thinking denotes a particular type of thinking. The precise meaning of rationality is a complex question beyond the scope of this analysis (though more will be said about it in chapter 2).[12] In the present context no injustice to rationality will result from simply construing it as the *intelligent use of all available evidence* for the solution of some problem. There are, of course, difficulties with the notion of evidence (what, for example, is to count as evidence?). Also, rationality may sometimes countenance the disregarding of certain types of evidence. But it is precisely from these problematic junctures in reasoning that critical thinking derives its conceptual content and it is here the employment of critical thinking is perhaps most useful. Indeed, it requires critical thinking even to recognize that one has arrived at such a juncture. All of this does not make critical thinking distinct from, much less incompatible with, rationality; rather rationality includes critical thinking as a particular aspect (or subset) of itself. The concept of critical thinking merely marks out the facet of rationality that comprises the disposition and skill to find such difficulties in the normal course of reasoning.

At this point perhaps it would be helpful to summarize the major features of critical thinking already identified.

1 Purporting to teach critical thinking in the abstract, in isolation from specific fields or problem areas, is muddled nonsense; thinking of any kind is always 'thinking about X'. Critical thinking cannot be a distinct subject.

2 The term 'critical thinking' has an identifiable meaning, but the criteria for its correct application vary from field to field.

3 Critical thinking does not necessarily entail disagreement with, rejection of or deviation from accepted norms.

4 The phrase 'reflective scepticism' captures the essence of the concept, but a more complete description would be something like 'the disposition and skill to do X in such a way that E (the available evidence from a field) is suspended (or temporarily rejected) as sufficient to establish the truth or viability of P (some proposition or action within X)'.

5 Critical thinking does not merely refer to the assessment of statements but includes the thought processes involved in problem solving and active engagement in certain activities.

6 The study of logic (both formal and informal) is by no means sufficient for thinking critically.

7 Insofar as critical thinking involves knowledge and skill, a critical thinker in area X might not be a critical thinker in area Y.

8 'Critical thinking' (like 'teaching' and 'education') is both a 'task' and an 'achievement' phrase, and does not necessarily imply success.

9 In addition to the assessment of statements, critical thinking may include the use (or rejection) of methods, strategies and techniques as exemplars.

10 Critical thinking is not coextensive with 'rationality' but is a dimension of it.

There are no doubt other dimensions of critical thinking upon which this analysis has not touched. But even this partial analysis of the concept can go some way towards clarifying much of the confusion and disagreement that surround discussions of critical thinking in relation to education, as we shall see in subsequent chapters.

The teachability of critical thinking

Having a working conception of what critical thinking is puts us in a better position to ask the question 'Is it teachable?' However, before we address this question head-on, let us consider what has come to be the dominant view or 'received opinion' about teaching critical thinking. It has already been pointed out that the many textbooks and articles on teaching critical thinking have focused largely upon the use of logic and the detection of fallacies. The rationale for this approach is that if students are familiar with the subtleties of logic (both formal and informal) and become skilled in its proper use, then they will at least know the rudiments of critical thinking, whether they choose to use this skill later or not. (Even the best of these materials are modest enough to recognize that you can lead the student to logic, but you can't make him use it!) This approach merely assumes that there is (or will be) a pervasive transfer of training across disciplinary boundaries. As with the similar claim made for the teaching of Latin, however, this assumption has never been substantiated. Indeed, there is evidence to the contrary.[13]

However, there is a much more serious deficiency in this approach to critical thinking than even the more modest of these proposals have recognized. Aside from my earlier point that there is no universal skill properly to be called critical thinking, there is an inherent limitation to the usefulness of logic in any problem-solving situation. The specific difficulty I have in mind has its parallel within the philosophy of science in the distinction between the 'context of discovery' and the 'context of justification'.[14] Very briefly, the context of discovery concerns those thought processes that are involved in forming (or generating) a hypothesis, whereas the context of justification is concerned with the acceptability of proofs of hypotheses once they have been put forward.[15] The logical positivists argued that the context of discovery was the exclusive domain of psychologists, sociologists and historians and not a domain for philosophy because there was (allegedly) no logic in this domain for philosophy to reconstruct. The context of justification, on the other hand, was an important domain for philosophy and logic since, being a rational process, it lent itself to 'rational reconstruction'. In this vein, Popper wrote:

> The initial stages, the act of conceiving or inventing a theory, seems to me neither to call for logical analysis nor to be susceptible of it. The question of how it happens that a new idea occurs to a man – whether it is a musical theme, a dramatic conflict, or a scientific theory – may be of great interest to empirical psychology; but it is irrelevant to the logical analysis of scientific knowledge.[16]

Elsewhere I have criticized this view[17] for making the distinction between discovery and justification too exclusive and also for overlooking a number of important philosophical problems in the context of discovery. However, there is one significant point for which the positivists must be given due credit, and that is that logic, as such, is used for the assessment and justification of arguments and theories once they have been presented. But it cannot generate (or formulate) hypotheses, theories or arguments in a problem-solving situation. It can only be used to verify those hypotheses. Having the tools of logic available to help us do this checking is valuable indeed; but they are virtually useless in helping us to find our way out of problematic situations the solutions to which depend on possibilities and hypotheses. Logic can help to eliminate hypotheses, conjectures and plausible solutions, but it cannot provide them. In the most common problem-solving situations within disciplines and working fields of knowledge, the most difficult – and perhaps most important – phase is that of producing a hypothesis, conjecture or alternative that is worth checking or trying out. As N. R. Hanson used to say, 'All cooking recipes for hare stew should begin with the prescription "First catch your hare!" ' In critical thinking we are, or should be, as much concerned with catching hares as we are with stewing them. Nowhere is this more evident than when we are teaching a student to learn a discipline or initiating him into a 'form of thought'. The most serious deficiency of teaching logic as a surrogate for critical thinking, then, is its virtual impotency in helping one to construct alternatives and possible solutions for oneself. And this is a necessity in all problem-solving situations. Logic can help a student to justify some thesis or argument, but it cannot help him discover one. One might object that logic is useful in helping us to solve problems because it enables us to eliminate incorrect hypotheses or poor solutions, thus bringing us closer to a solution. I would not deny this. But logic cannot initiate or propose hypotheses (or putative solutions); the problem-solver must construct them for himself. Moreover, the ingredient that renders any putative solution plausible in the first place is not logic but knowledge and information from within the field or problem area. The deficiencies of logic in the context of critical thinking, and of our understanding of the context of discovery in general, are clearly expressed in a statement made by David Bakan criticizing research practices in psychology:

> There is nothing intrinsically wrong with the emphasis upon the testing of hypotheses. It is an important part of the total investigatory enterprise. What I do wish to point out, however, is that by the time the investigatory enterprise has reached the state of testing hypotheses, most of the important work, if there has been any, has already been done. One is tempted to think that psychologists are often like children playing cowboys; they emulate them in everything but their main work, which is taking care of cows. The main work of scientists is thinking and making discoveries of what was not thought beforehand. Psychologists often attempt to 'play scientist' by avoiding the main work.[18]

Similarly, logic texts often 'play at critical thinking' by avoiding the main work, which is solving problems in the context of discovery.

Even those few prescriptions that logic can offer to the problem solver (for example, avoiding ambiguities, question begging, contradictions and so on) are all so general, and frequently so obvious, that they are virtually useless for solving problems. The most advanced literature on general problem solving,[19] which relies heavily on heuristic devices (rules of thumb learned by trial and error) and is therefore more flexible than logic, is quite open about the limitations of heuristics in general. It is axiomatic that the more general the area of application for any heuristic, the less precise its suggested solutions and hence its heuristic power. For example, one such general heuristic is: 'Suggest classes which contain plausible hypotheses by looking at the most significant features of the data.'[20] But such a suggestion begs all the interesting and difficult questions that face the working problem solver, such as how does one know which features are the most 'significant', or which class of hypotheses is the most 'plausible'? The correct answer to these questions should be that one learns these things by learning the discipline in which the problem arises, not by taking courses in problem-solving, critical thinking or logic.

This brings us back to our question about the teachability of critical thinking. I have suggested that critical thinking involves both a propensity and a skill. Both are necessary because neither one by itself would be sufficient to capture what is normally meant by referring to someone as a 'critical thinker'. Thus teaching someone to be a critical thinker entails both the cognitive and affective domains of a student's learning in an area. While conscientious teachers hope that their results will transfer to other areas, they should be content with success in their own area, since there is little reason to believe that the required skills in other areas will be exactly the same. And if the students' propensity carries over where they do not have the skill, they are likely to embarrass themselves: as Socrates suggested, a little learning is a dangerous thing.

Even within some specific area of learning, at least two distinguishable tasks confront the teacher who is trying to promote critical thinking. On the one hand, he is *teaching how*, which issues in procedures or skills; and on the other, he is *teaching to*, which issues in dispositions, propensities, or tendencies.[21] And the things that the teacher does to achieve the one might not be sufficient for achieving the other. In short, he is trying to provide the student with both a capacity and the will to use it. I do not think that John Passmore's referring to this combination as a 'character trait'[22] is particularly helpful, since a character trait seems to consist in a more general disposition that applies across a wide variety of endeavours. In addition, a character trait connotes something more or less immutable in one's personality that is largely affective in nature.

To the extent that critical thinking is a skill, it is teachable in much the same way that other skills are teachable, namely, through drills, exercises or problem solving in an area. However, teachers have been assigning exercises and drills for years without achieving the desired result. Thus it is clear that merely providing exercises is not sufficient. A much clearer understanding of the proper types of problems and exercises needs to be reached not only by teachers but also by the educational community as a whole. No doubt students' understanding of what is expected of them will also affect the success of such endeavours. But insofar as critical thinking does involve skills, that part of it at least is in principle directly teachable. I would add, however, that because there is no universal skill nor curriculum subject that is properly called critical thinking, it should therefore be taught as an integral part of other subjects. Not to do so is like teaching a person to type on a typewriter with an unknown alphabet a language that is foreign to him: love's labour is largely lost.

When the principles of, and methods for, teaching the skills of critical thinking are understood, however, there remains the problem of getting students to use these skills, of ensuring that they become part of the students' normal intellectual repertoire. Something in the attitude of the teacher or the atmosphere of the classroom must influence the student to become personally disposed to use these skills. Suggestions for various ways and means for influencing people's preferences and dispositions are numerous. Getting people to think critically may in fact be like getting them to act morally. Long ago Aristotle suggested that the way to get people to X (dispositionally) was to provide them with good examples to follow. More recently Jerome Bruner has suggested that when students come to see the 'power' of various principles and ideas, they will use them. I am sure that such suggestions have considerable merit and are at least partially correct. The final answer to this question, however, will be largely on empirical matter and cannot be settled here. It is sufficient for our purposes to recognize that training in particular critical thinking skills is not sufficient to produce a critical thinker. One must also develop the disposition to use those skills.

Conclusion

This chapter has attempted to dispel much of what I think has been muddled and mistaken in most treatments of critical thinking. The proliferation of courses and texts on critical thinking and informal logic appears to demand clarification of precisely what it is that they are purporting to teach. As a start, I have suggested that critical thinking is the appropriate use of reflective scepticism, and that this is necessarily linked with specific areas of expertise and knowledge. However, much more needs to be said, since the present analysis has provided only a skeletal framework for a more complete understanding of critical thinking. That understanding can best be reached by considering its function in education generally.

NOTES

1. Robert H. Ennis, 'A concept of critical thinking', *Harvard Educational Review*, vol. 32, no. 1 (Winter, 1962), pp. 83–111. I shall have more to say on Ennis's views on critical thinking later.
2. For a good introduction to this literature, see P. C. Wason and P. N. Johnson-Laird (eds.), *Thinking and Reasoning* (Harmondsworth: Penguin, 1970). Several of the papers provide extensive bibliographies.

3. Michael Polanyi has argued, in his *Personal Knowledge: Towards a Post-Critical Philosophy* (New York: Harper and Row, 1962), p. 264, that the adjectives 'critical' and 'uncritical' apply only to the deliberate process of granting acceptance or rejection of an idea.

4. For an analysis of 'creative' in the context of education, see J. P. White's 'Creativity and education: a philosophical analysis', in Jane R. Martin (ed.), *Readings in the Philosophy of Education: A Study of Curriculum* (Boston: Allyn and Bacon Inc., 1970), pp. 122–37.

5. 'On teaching to be critical', in R. S. Peters (ed.), *The Concept of Education*, (London: Routledge and Kegan Paul, 1967), p. 193.

6. John Passmore has clearly argued 'On teaching to be critical' that critical thinking is not a habit as such, nor is it merely a skill. My comments would show that I agree with this.

7. 'A concept of critical thinking', p. 84.

8. *ibid.*

9. The distinction I am drawing here is commensurate with what Abraham Kaplan has called 'logic-in-use' *versus* 'reconstructed logic' in *The Conduct of Inquiry* (San Francisco: Chandler, 1964), pp. 3–17.

10. I think Jane Roland Martin has more or less obliterated Ryle's initial distinction between 'knowing how' and 'knowing that' in her *Explaining, Understanding, and Teaching* (New York: McGraw-Hill, 1970), pp. 146–52, showing among other things that each involves significant components of the other. See also her 'On the reduction of "knowing that" to "knowing how"', in B. O. Smith and R. H. Ennis (eds.), *Language and Concepts in Education* (Chicago: Rand McNally, 1961), pp. 59–71.

11. *Personal Knowledge*, pp. 49–65.

12. For an excellent beginning to the contemporary literature on 'rationality', see Bryan R. Wilson (ed.), *Rationality* (New York: Harper and Row, 1970).

13. For a clear-headed discussion of this evidence, see Bryce B. Hudgins, *Learning and Thinking* (Itasca, Ill.: F. E. Peacock, 1978).

14. This distinction was first articulated by Hans Reichenbach in his *Experience and Prediction* (Chicago: University of Chicago Press, 1938), and continued to be used by Karl Popper in *The Logic of Scientific Discovery* (New York: Harper and Row, 1968).

15. For a lengthy discussion of this distinction, see my 'A logic of discovery: lessons from history and current prospects', unpublished Ph.D. dissertation, *Dissertation Abstracts*, University of Michigan Microfilms (Ann Arbor, Michigan), 1973.

16. *The Logic of Scientific Discovery*, p. 31.

17. 'The context of discovery in context', *Proceedings of XV World Congress of Philosphy*, Varna, Bulgaria, 1973, Book III. See also my 'A logic of discovery', pp. 1–33.

18. *On Method: Toward a Reconstruction of Psychological Investigation*, (San Francisco, 1968), p. 44.

19. This literature is now vast, but a good introduction to it is E. Feigenbaum and J. Feldman (eds.), *Computers and Thought* (New York:

McGraw-Hill, 1963); see also A. Newell, J. Shaw, and H. Simon, *Elements of a Theory of Human Problem Solving*, Paper P-971, the Rand Corp. (Santa Monica, 1957); M. L. Minksy, 'Some methods of artificial intelligence and heuristic programming', in *Mechanization of Thought Processes* (London: HMSO, 1959); A. Newell 'Heuristic programming: ill-structured problems', to appear in *Progress in Operations Research* (in press); B. Kleinmuntz (ed.), *Problem Solving: Research, Method and Theory* (New York: Krieger, 1965).

20. C. West Churchman and Bruce G. Buchanan, 'On the design of inductive systems: some philosophical problems', to appear in D. Michie *et al.* (eds.) *Machine Intelligence* (in press).

21. This conforms to two of the four types of learning that Jonas Soltis has distinguished (learning *that*, learning *how to*, learning *to* and states of attainment like 'appreciation') in his 'Analysis and anomalies in philosophy of education', unpublished paper presented at the Conference on New Directions in Philosophy of Education, held at the Ontario Institute for Studies in Education, Toronto, 30 April–2 May 1970.

22. 'On teaching to be critical', pp. 195–7; in general, however, this is an excellent paper.

CHAPTER 2

Critical Thinking, Epistemology and Education

Because the educationally concerned public bemoans the lack of critical thinking ability in our students, it is generally inclined to accept proposals for formal courses in logic or critical thinking. That would appear to be the most natural way to scratch this kind of itch. What this same public does not seem to realize, however, is that the real problem with uncritical students is not a deficiency in a general skill, such as logical ability, but rather a more general lack of education in the traditional sense. In the present chapter I shall attempt to show why courses in logic fail to accomplish the goal of developing critical thinkers and how the epistemology of various subjects would be the most reasonable route to that end. Ironically, as it turns out, the epistemological approach to critical thinking involves little more than providing what has always been a necessary condition of education, namely, understanding what constitutes good reasons for various beliefs. In short, there is both a conceptual and a pedagogic link between epistemology, critical thinking and education, but the study of logic or critical thinking as such has no part in this linkage.

In chapter 1 the point was made that the concept of critical thinking is not restricted to the assessment of statements or propositional contexts, but also extends to such things as decisions, skills, methods and techniques. This broader view of the range of critical thinking represents a departure from most textbook accounts of critical thinking. In this chapter, however, I too shall restrict my discussion to the assessment of statements, since this is the prime area of interest in most academic subjects. The standard approach for developing critical thinking in this context has been to teach logic and various kinds of general reasoning skills. Presumably, the rationale for this approach is that since logic plays a role in every subject, and logic is intimately related to reasoning, the study of logic should improve one's ability to assess arguments and statements in any subject area. What I wish to argue is that the plausibility of this reasoning can be sustained only by seriously underestimating the complexity of the different kinds of information used in arguments and by overestimating the role of logic in these assessments. That is, even when the problem at issue is the rational assessment of some statement or argument, the major requirements for such assessment are epistemological, not logical, in character.

My use of the term 'epistemological' harbours nothing exotic. It refers simply to the analysis of good reasons for various beliefs. Ideally, of course, epistemology attempts to provide the very best reasons for holding a belief, and to this extent its purpose is identical with that of rationality. The best reasons, however, need not involve logical certainty in the logician's sense. In many fields of inquiry outside mathematics and logic we must rely upon, and be content with, less stringent criteria for 'good reasons'. Just as there are different kinds of knowledge, so there are different kinds of reasons, evidence and modes of justifying them. What might be a good reason for one kind of belief could be an extremely bad *type* of reason to support another kind of belief. When we say of someone that he has learned to understand a particular discipline or field of study we are saying, among other things, that he appreciates what constitutes a good reason in that area. We should notice, however, that a minimal condition for understanding a good reason in any field is that one understands the full meaning of the specialized and often technical language in which such reasons are expressed. That is, an understanding of the semantic content of a field-dependent proposition is a prerequisite for its assessment. This basic understanding is necessary whether the object of assessment is an entire argument or a singular statement. Indeed, it is this straightforward, semantic dimension of the assessment of statements and arguments that I wish to stress as the most important, most difficult and most fruitful area to pursue for the development of critical thinking in any field. I refer to this kind of emphasis as 'epistemological' because it has far more to do with the meanings (or semantic content) of statements than with the logical (or syntactic) relations between propositions. In a proposition, for example, that is expressed as $P \rightarrow Q$ it is far more important and more complex to understand what P or Q *mean* than to understand the syntactic relation between P and Q (expressed by the symbol $\rightarrow$); hence my basic departure from the logic approach to critical thinking.

I should point out, moreover, that the use of the term 'epistemology' here is not restricted to the simple meanings of words in the sense of dictionary definitions. Rather, it includes understanding concepts and the peculiarities of the nature of evidence, as they are understood by practitioners in the field from which they emanate. For example, both the term 'mass' and the corresponding sentence 'The mass will expand' have entirely different meanings in the contexts of physics and Marxist political theory. Both meanings make sense in their respective contexts, but both have entirely different connotations and denotations. What is of importance here, though, is that an adequate understanding of these different concepts and their definitions typically requires an understanding of still other concepts and evidence that may also be peculiar to that field. In sum, while for me epistemology simply means the analysis of good reasons for belief, understanding the various kinds of reason involves understanding complex meanings of field-dependent concepts and evidence.

The logic approach to critical thinking simply bypasses these epistemological considerations by treating information generally as 'mere information' – as though it could always be found and understood simply by consulting an almanac or encyclopaedia. In logic, information and statements conveying it are merely values or place-holders for the Ps and Qs, which are then to be manipulated with logical rules. Indeed, training in these rules constitutes its major, if not its sole, contribution to critical thinking. In my view, by contrast, such things as the tacit rules of evidence and the meanings of concepts are the major determinants for the proper assessment of statements and arguments. In order to appreciate this point, however, it might be useful to look at some of the more familiar situations in which critical thinking might be called for and in which the logic approach purports to be most useful.

Can logic improve practical reason?

It seems that every time one turns around there is some new public issue on which the Government is asking us to vote in a plebiscite or referendum. If the issue is not a new nuclear power station or the banning of a product, it is a new tax-reform measure or an amendment to a law. Occasionally, as a responsible citizen, I do my best to 'get to the bottom' of some of these issues so that I may vote with 'knowledge' as distinct from mere political opinion. And I am invariably struck by (or, more accurately, disappointed at) how dependent I am on the knowledge and technical information of various experts and how very little my formal study of logic and critical thinking actually helps in resolving these questions. Real issues of this sort turn out not to be at all like the contrived exercises in the logic texts, in which all the relevant information is given and the truth of the premises can be assumed. Rather, in deciding upon real public questions it is usually not the logical validity of an argument that we find difficult but rather the task of determining whether certain premises are in fact true. And this latter difficulty invariably takes us into the unfamiliar ground of some technical subject area, where each question seems to generate several others and epistemological uncertainties abound. And where expert testimony appears to conflict, perhaps because it is based upon different theories, our quandary worsens.

One of the difficulties associated with making such decisions is that there is simply a very large amount of information that needs to be processed. This difficulty can arise in connection with any issue, familiar or not, but the most striking problem with these unfamiliar realms of expertise is that they presuppose a knowledge of technical language and an epistemological framework that the uninitiated cannot possess. It is not the quantity of evidence that gives us trouble in these cases; it is its quality. If, for example, the question at issue has a legal aspect, we may find that truth as such is quite beside the point. Issues involving an amendment to the Constitution may require technical knowledge gleaned from political science or jurisprudence, not to mention knowledge of the historical purpose and terms of reference of the Constitution. Even in familiar tax-reform issues, we need to know something about economics, sliding financial scales, municipal funding and perhaps other areas of expertise in which we are not even sure what counts as a 'good reason' for a belief or decision.

Ironically, it is for the examination of public issues such as the above that introductory logic texts claim to be most useful. Their examples are invariably drawn from newspaper editorials, letters to the editor, political speeches or media accounts of public issues. But the logic approach to these issues totally ignores the epistemological problems associated with the special knowledge that bears upon these issues. The result is too often superficial opinion masquerading as profound insight into complex public issues.

Even in the supposedly simple textbook examples of reasoning to conclusions I am struck by how much of the reasoning depends upon specific technical information. Consider two arbitrarily selected examples from one such textbook.[1] Without additional information, the student is instructed:

Explain why each of the following analogical arguments is inductively strong or why it is not:

1. Robert Tryon's experiments with breeding rats make it probable that selective breeding (eugenics) affects intelligence in rats. What we know about heredity indicates that rats and humans share a number of hereditary principles. Thus it seems probable that eugenics would affect intelligence in humans too.

      . . . . .

3. Regularly taking LSD has great adverse physical effects. Since marijuana is a hallucinogen like LSD, it too probably produces great adverse physical effects.

If the information given in each example is in fact true and no other information is necessary to assess these arguments, then I would argue that they both might be either strong or weak. But the 'correct' answers given at the end of the chapter are respectively:

1. This argument is inductively strong. The mechanism of heredity is basically the same for all animals including man. Thus rats and man share a number of properties relevant to the inferred property. Given what we know about heredity, it appears as if there are few if any relevant dissimilarities. Since a large number of rats were tested and we know of no animals that share the same heredity principles and yet lack the inferred property, the conclusion of the argument is probable.

      . . . . . .

3. The argument is inductively weak. The only common property mentioned is that LSD and marijuana are hallucinogens. There are relevant dissimilarities too. LSD is much more potent than marijuana. Thus the argument as it stands is weak.

Notice, however, the extent to which the author is constrained to add technical information in order to make (I do not say 'show') his case. The assessment of the arguments as weak or strong cannot stand on its own without further information, and the student is placed in the unenviable position of having to assess them without the necessary information. Nor can such examples be defended on grounds that the additional information needed is mere common sense or common knowledge, because the whole purpose of such exercises in logic is to show that it is something in the *form* of arguments, as distinct from their content, that makes them strong or weak. If a student believed all hallucinogens to be dangerous (as various poisons are) or that rats' maze-running ability is decidedly different from human intelligence (which is plausible), then his or her assessment of the strength of these arguments could correctly be the exact opposite of the author's.

What these examples show, I think, is that typically we are in a quandary less about the logical validity of an argument than about the truth of the putative evidence. We frequently cannot determine whether evidence is good or not, because such a judgement depends upon special knowledge. One has to be a fellow participant in the particular domain of meaning to appreciate the proper significance of the evidence. Indeed, the domain of inquiry from which the evidence comes might be one in which familiar canons of logic do not apply. Examples of such domains are not restricted to art, religion or morals either, but could also include quantum physics, economics, law and innumerable other areas of inquiry. Nor are such domains epistemologically deficient in any way because the normal canons of logic are not sufficient. It is rather that within different fields, different sorts of reasons can (and do) count as good reasons. The significance of this observation has, by and large, been overlooked by the proponents of logic for critical thinking. But its implications for critical thinking go beyond anything that logic, *per se*, can rectify.

On the different types of question

Another symptom of the extent to which the logic

approach to critical thinking devalues and minimizes information is the special importance it assigns to the 'conceptual *versus* empirical' distinction. Clearly, it is important to know whether one is addressing oneself to an empirical question or a conceptual one, since this will determine what kind of analysis is most appropriate. If, for example, a statement or argument is alleged to be true by virtue of its form alone, then conceptual analysis and deductive logic are the proper tools to use. On the other hand, if a statement or argument is intended to be a report of facts, then observation and inductive logic are the appropriate analytical tools. It is not surprising, therefore, that this distinction should serve as the initial lesson to be learned in the logic approach to critical thinking. One of my objections to this approach, however, is that it often turns out to be the final lesson as well.

Since most arguments are (arguably) either deductive or inductive, and the logic approach features the ability to use logic, this approach derives its appeal from its apparent power to cover virtually any situation requiring analysis. All one needs do, the instructions say, is to determine what kind of statement or argument one is dealing with and then put the appropriate logical tools to work. However, this approach has two significant shortcomings, which render its general power more apparent than real. The first is that it assumes that a student, or indeed anyone, will generally be able to recognize when he is confronted with a conceptual question and when an empirical one. But questions, statements and arguments do not come ready-labelled with identity tags, and it is often difficult for accomplished logicians to make this determination with any certainty.[2] One of the main reasons why it is difficult to make such determinations is that the task frequently requires specialized knowledge of the field from which a question or statement arises. And even within fields of inquiry it is not always well established which kind of statement is which. There was, for example, some dispute within the science of entomology as to whether the proposition 'Spiders have eight legs' was to be regarded as an empirical observation or a conceptual truth. The issue was finally resolved by defining all eight-legged insects as 'spiders', just as the property of being unmarried is a defining characteristic of a 'bachelor'. There is also a controversy of the same type in modern physics about the logical status of the statement 'Water boils at 100°C'. Is this an empirical statement or a conceptual truth? Whatever the answer, no amount of training in logic will provide it.

A second shortcoming of the excessive importance assigned to the 'conceptual *versus* empirical' distinction is that it masks significant differences within each category (of propositions), which are greater than the difference between the categories. Consider, for example, the following pairs of sentences.

1   Organisms respond to stimuli. [Presently a conceptual truth]
2   Which particular stimuli will organism X respond to? [An empirical question]

The difference in cognitive requirements for understanding the above sentences, even though one is conceptual and the other empirical, is far less than that required for answering the following questions.

3   Could improved spectrographic methods ever measure the core temperature of a star? [An empirical question]
4   Can you see any stars tonight? [Another empirical question]

While 3 and 4 are of the same logical type (namely, empirical), the difference in the cognitive requirements for understanding them is far greater than that between 1 and 2. The degrees of complexity within and among empirical information are virtually infinite. A programme for developing critical thinking that does not take adequate account of these huge differences risks sanctioning a very superficial understanding of the different types of knowledge and cognitive skills required for critical thinking. Reliance upon the 'conceptual *versus* empirical' distinction and the deductive *versus* inductive' distinction tends to obscure these fundamental differences. Both the aforementioned shortcomings are direct consequences of minimizing the role of information and its complexities, which is an inherent characteristic of the logic approach to critical thinking.

On the existence of different logics

One of the practical implications of my view of the requirements for effective critical thinking is that one must come to understand the basic concepts and epistemological foundations of a wide range of fields. And, clearly, this implies a considerable amount of particularized study in this wide range of fields. By contrast, the *prima facie* appeal of the logic approach is that it promises a generalized critical thinking skill by teaching just one or at most two logical systems. Thus the economics of effort clearly appear to favour the logic approach to critical thinking. However, setting aside, for the moment, my general epistemological objections to this view, there are serious internal difficulties that should make one question its general effectiveness. Indeed, these difficulties stem from the growing field of logic itself.

During the last 125 years we have witnessed the development of many diverse logics: Boolean and non-Boolean algebras, multivalued logics, modal logics, deontic logics, quantum logics and decision-theoretic models of reasoning. In each of these logics the notion of validity is relatively defined according to the rules of inference that are peculiar to itself. Formation rules and rules of detachment are designed to do certain kinds of work by sanctioning some inferences and prohibiting others. The very proliferation of these logics testifies to the fact that different areas of human inquiry require different methods of validation. No single logical system can capture the validation procedures of every discipline, nor all the problem areas within a single discipline. Reasoning in particular problem areas is often *sui generis*, and the range of human experience is too diverse to allow us to hope, much less think, that a single logic or two could capture all such reasoning.

What, one might ask, is the significance of so many logics for critical thinking? Perhaps the most obvious implication is that formalism (hence the logic approach) is no longer viable, if it ever was, as a means of providing a singular, universal standard for rational belief. This can be seen from the fact that even within the domain of formal systems as such, there are, and need to be, alternative definitions of validity and rational inference. And when we move away from formal modes of reasoning into various empirical domains the hope of a universal standard of rational inference becomes even dimmer.

Indeed, considerations such as these prompted Stephen Toulmin, among others, to defend the view that each field of research has its own internal logic, Toulmin argues:

> What has to be recognized first is that validity is an intra-field, not an inter-field notion. Arguments within any field can be judged by standards appropriate within that field, and some will fall short; but it must be expected that the standards will be field-dependent, and that the merits to be demanded of an argument in one field will be found to be absent (in the nature of things) from entirely meritorious arguments in another.[3]

The defenders of the logic approach might be tempted to respond to this by pointing out that whatever standards of validity are used to assess arguments, those standards will still be logical in character. Hence, they might argue, the need for logic has not been reduced by these considerations. I think, however, that this response relies more heavily on an apparent connotation of the word 'logic' than its denotation will effectively support. It is quite true that the use of the word 'logic' implies some formal, or at least public, standards of validity. But if these standards of validity are in fact different from one another, then the logics are different, and there may be little more than a loose family resemblance between them that prompts us to call them all 'logic'. For all practical purposes, however, one would have to learn each logic separately – just as one has to learn the field-dependent concepts of each field differently. From this point of view, the need to learn the logic of each field is on a par with the need to learn their epistemologies: in both cases there is a proliferation of different subjects to be studied. According to Toulmin, moreover, it is clear that the differences between logics are just as pronounced:

> We must learn to tolerate in comparative logic a state of affairs long taken for granted in comparative anatomy. A man, a monkey, a pig or a porcupine – to say nothing of a frog, a herring, a thrush and a coelacanth – each will be found to have its own anatomical structure: limbs, bones, organs and tissues arranged in a pattern characteristic of its species. In each species, some individuals will be deformed, either lacking an organ needed for life and survival, or having a part which is prevented by its make-up from serving the creature's life in a fully effective way. Yet what in an individual of one species counts as deformation may represent normality in one of another. A man with a hand the shape of a monkey's would indeed be deformed, and handicapped in living a man's life; but the very features which handicapped the man might be indispensible to the ape – far from being deformities, they could be of positive advantage. In this sense, normality and deformity are 'intra-specific', not 'inter-specific' notions, and the same kind of situation holds for terms of logical assessment. If we ask about the validity, necessity, rigour or impossibility of arguments or conclusions, we must ask these questions within the limits of a given field, and avoid, as it were, condemning an ape for not being a man or a pig for not being a porcupine.[4]

It is clear from this that Toulmin is defending a view of the differences between subject matter that we might call the 'strong' view, since it holds that each field may have its own unique logic. According to this view, it would make little sense to talk about learning logic *simpliciter*, but only the logic of this field or that. And it could turn out that there are as many logics as there are distinguishable fields. Up to this point, however, I have advanced a somewhat 'weaker' view, which holds only that, for the purposes of critical thinking, we should consider each field of inquiry to have its own peculiar epistemology. Thus, where the 'strong' view claims that there are significant syntactical differences that distinguish discrete fields, I am merely claiming that there are (at least) significant semantic and epistemic differences that distinguish them. Both views clearly imply that there is no single or monolithic route to effective critical thinking for all, or even most, fields.

The relationship between critical thinking and education

This chapter began by suggesting that there was a conceptual link between critical thinking, epistemology and education. Since the above discussion was designed to show how epistemology and critical thinking are related, all that remains is to show how these notions are related to education. I think it important to show this connection because there has been considerable confusion over the precise role, if any, of critical thinking in various school programmes.

In general, I think it is fair to say that the connection between critical thinking and education is far more intimate and more important than even the proponents of critical thinking courses have recognized. Normally, critical thinking courses have marginal curricular status and are, at best, tacked on to existing programmes as a kind of dietary supplement for 'enrichment'. For the moment I do not want to discuss the practical and administrative questions of the precise manner in which critical thinking should be inserted into the curriculum: I will turn to that later. What I am concerned to show here is the logical relationship between the concept of critical thinking and the concept of education. And what I shall argue is not only that it would be a good thing if our educational institutions could get students to be critical thinkers, but also that, insofar as the purpose of schools is to educate, this task logically cannot be accomplished without critical thinking. In short, critical thinking is a necessary condition for education.

Whatever else an analysis of education might reveal, it surely entails the acquisition of knowledge. Conceptual analysts and curriculum theorists might argue over the various types of knowledge that form constituents of education, but I can think of no one who would seriously doubt that knowledge of some sort is entailed by eduction. Moreover, an analysis of knowledge will reveal that the knower must be in possession of a justification for that which is putatively known. In the *Theaetetus* Plato first argued that knowledge consisted of 'true belief, plus an account' (200D–201C). Contemporary analyses render this same view somewhat more formally, as follows:[5]

> S knows P
> if and only if:
> (i)   S believes P,
> (ii)   S has adequate evidence of P,
> and (iii)   P is true.

The important point of this analysis of knowledge is that one must have a justification for one's belief in order to distinguish knowledge from mere true opinion. One is not entitled to claim to know something, even if true, unless one can produce the justification that supports the belief. A common criticism of school learning is that students learn 'facts', perhaps by rote or because 'the teacher says so', without acquiring the corresponding evidence and arguments that support those 'facts'. The result is opinion passing as knowledge and wisdom. This common criticism is merely an elliptical way of recognizing that knowledge involves the justification of one's beliefs, and that students frequently lack such justification.

The process of justifying one's beliefs, however, has two distinguishable dimensions. One is to assess the veracity and internal validity of the evidence as presented, and the other is to judge whether the belief, together with its supporting evidence, is compatible with an existing belief system. If it is not compatible, then an adjustment somewhere in the system will be required: there is something amiss either with the new evidence or with the system of beliefs.[6] The importance of this process of assessing, fitting and adjusting beliefs cannot be overemphasized because it is this process that makes the belief 'belong' to a person as distinct from being merely a proposition or belief that he knows about. Without this personal assessment process, a student might recite a certain proposition, together with its attendant evidence, yet still not be justified in holding the belief because it conflicts with other beliefs he holds. Coherence within one's belief system may or may not be sufficient to establish ultimate truth, but it is certainly a necessary condition of rationality; and one is not justified in holding a belief unless this necessary condition is met.

Thus the process of integrating a belief or new piece of evidence into one's overall belief system is part of the justification process; one must perceive the appropriate connections between the available evidence and the belief system. But most important from the point of view of knowledge, the connection(s) between the evidence and the belief must constitute one's reason for believing it. (This is because it is logically possible for a person to believe P and be in possession of adequate evidence for P, yet not to believe P for *that* reason; he might believe P because of some longstanding prejudice for example. I think, therefore, that this required dimension of knowledge might be adequately captured by adding a further condition to the standard analyses of knowledge, as follows:

> S knows P
> if and only if:
> (i)   S believes P,
> (ii)   S has adequate evidence of P,
> (iii) The evidence constitutes S's reason for believing P,
> and (iv)   P is true.

The addition of this new condition (iii) rules out the case (or possibility) of the student who may be familiar with the evidence only in the sense that he can compliantly recite it by rote. This new condition requires that justified beliefs be a direct function of the evidence, which is something demanded by our intuitions about knowledge.

It is possible to argue, of course, that the notion of adequate evidence already carries with it the implication that the belief and its attendant evidence is compatible with the existing belief system, else it would not be adequate. I see no formal objection to construing the notion of adequate evidence in this general way. It does leave buried, however, the very real problems associated with integrating one's beliefs and experience, such as turning the objective evidence (that is, the inductive probabilities) into one's reason for believing it (that is, the epistemic probabilities). In this regard, Michael Polanyi has argued that turning so-called 'facts' into 'personal knowledge' is the most critical, yet most neglected, problem facing contemporary epistemology.[7] Idiosyncratic belief states of different individuals determine in important ways what facts can and will be accepted as *bona fide* additions to the belief system.

Whichever way one chooses to construe the analysis of knowledge, however, it is quite clear that knowledge, by definition, presupposes some sort of justification. And arriving at a justification requires the agent to suspend a given belief long enough to assess the internal coherence of the evidence for it and to integrate the belief within his existing belief system. But to say that a temporary suspension of judgement is required for justifying one's beliefs is simply another way of saying that one must be self-critical or possess a critical mind with respect to P in order to produce a justification. Thus the integration and internalization of beliefs and evidence require critical thinking. Moreover, critical thinking, as I have argued, involves just such a suspension of belief.

Critical thinking then, is not just a frill or dietary supplement to be added to education, but is logically entailed by it. Some of the popular critics of education have been correct: critical thinking can improve education. What has not been sufficiently recognized, however, is that education absolutely requires it. The question 'What is the connection between education and critical thinking?' has now been answered: the connection is one of logical entailment. Critical thinking must, therefore, command a place in any institution committed to the pursuit of education because critical thinking is a necessary condition of it.

With this general understanding of what critical

thinking is (and is not) and its relation to education, we can now turn to some of the major proposals that have appeared for its promulgation.

NOTES

1. David B. Annis, *Techniques of Critical Reasoning* (Columbus, Ohio: Charles E. Merrill, 1974), p. 86.
2. W. V. O. Quine has argued that this distinction is, at bottom, arbitrary anyway. What is to count as a conceptual truth and what an empirical one is ultimately determined by convention. See his 'Two dogmas of empiricism', in *From a Logical Point of View* (New York: Harper and Row, 1963).
3. Stephen Toulmin, *The Uses of Argument* (Cambridge: Cambridge University Press, 1958), p. 255.
4. *ibid.*, p. 256.
5. This analysis appears in more literature than is worth detailing here. But an excellent discussion of this analysis of knowledge, particularly in relation to education, can be found in Israel Scheffler's *The Conditions of Knowledge* (Glenview, Ill.: Scott, Foresman, 1965).
6. I am referring here to the problem of turning what logicians call an 'inductive probability' into an 'epistemic probability'. See Brian Skyrms, *Choice and Chance* (Belmont, Cal.: Dickenson, 1966), pp. 15–18.
7. See his *Personal Knowledge: Towards a Post-Critical Philosophy* (New York: Harper and Row, 1962), pp. 249–59.

CHAPTER 3

The Prevailing View of the Concept of Critical Thinking

> To imagine that thinking can be broken down
> into its component parts which are then
> programmed is to misunderstand the nature
> of thinking.[1]

There are many programmes for teaching critical thinking already extant in the schools. My purpose here is to examine the theoretical foundation upon which many of these programmes are predicated.

Just a cursory glance at some of the espoused rationales reveals a point of view marked by a naive form of logical positivism – a view that has been largely abandoned or severely qualified by most philosophers today. For example, many analyses of the concept of critical thinking are replete with lists of skills that serve tacitly as operational definitions of the concept and with lists of pitfalls to be avoided, as though these could be exhaustively anticipated in advance. In addition, there is a not-so-subtle subscription to the verifiability criterion of meaning and the repeated employment in crucial places of the fact/value distinction, as though it were non-controversial and clearly demarcated. But perhaps the most pervasive notion underlying these analyses is what amounts to an unquestioned faith in the efficacy of science and its methods to settle every significant controversy requiring critical thought.

Robert Ennis's analysis

If one traces the recent origins of this sort of view, through references and explicit citations, it is clear that Robert Ennis's paper 'A concept of critical thinking' has been most influential.[2] When the paper was published in 1962 there was a paucity of literature analysing the concept in such a manner that educators could directly teach, and psychologists accurately test, critical thinking. As Ennis says:

> The main task of this paper is to present a clear and detailed account of a concept of *critical thinking*. This account can be judged for its defensibility, and if found defensible, can serve as a basis for research in the teaching of and testing for critical thinking ability.[3]

Judging from the direction of subsequent teaching and research efforts, it appears that Ennis's paper had the intended effect. This is not to suggest that Ennis's analysis was adopted without qualification by subsequent researchers, but that it formed a general framework around which subsequent efforts have tended to build.

It is important to be as clear as possible about what Ennis was trying to do in this paper, because even careful study of the paper leaves his actual intent anything but evident. For example, it is never clear whether Ennis sees himself as providing a conceptual analysis of critical thinking, so that we can know more clearly what it is, or merely a list of suggestive 'aspects' of critical thinking that researchers and educators ought to use as discrete and testable foci. While these two endeavours are distinct, there is considerable evidence throughout the paper that Ennis sees himself as providing both. Regardless of his intent, I shall argue that the analysis fails on both counts, but it is disquieting not to know at what point precisely he is trying to carry out which.[4] It would seem, in such circumstances, that the most charitable course would be to interpret what Ennis says from both perspectives, at least where this is possible, and to evaluate it separately in each case.

Ennis's paper is entitled 'A concept of critical thinking', and not 'The concept of critical thinking', which suggests that he is going to outline one possible view. The initial abstract, however, describes him as 'identifying twelve aspects of critical thinking', with the clear implication that these have been discovered through analysis. This kind of ambiguity of purpose is pervasive even in the first few pages, where Ennis is telling the reader explicitly what he is going to do. One thing that is clear to both the reader and Ennis, however, is that his thesis has three distinguishable parts or components:

1   the basic concept of critical thinking, which he defines as 'the correct assessing of statements';
2   twelve 'aspects' (sometimes called 'abilities') that 'come under the basic notion of *critical thinking* as the correct assessing of statements';
3   three distinguishable dimensions of critical thinking: a logical dimension, a criterial dimension and a pragmatic dimension.

Ennis admits that various lists of 'aspects' or 'abilities' for critical thinking have appeared in the literature before (and since), but his original contribution consists in the basic concept of critical thinking (1 above) and his 'dimensional simplification' (3 above). I shall examine all three components, but I shall focus primarily on the two original ones, since, presumably, they account for the paper's wide influence.

The opening paragraphs of Ennis's paper are spent reviewing the paucity and relative deficiencies of research in critical thinking. In addition to explaining why this is the case in psychology, he criticizes Dewey's attempts in this direction by stating that his work on problem solving 'unfortunately suggests that the problem is solved when the solver thinks it is solved, thus providing a psychological instead of a logical criterion for the solution of a problem.'[5] In an attempt to resolve these longstanding deficiencies, Ennis thus presents his definition of critical thinking as 'the correct assessing of statements'. While this definition seems plausible enough, one still wants to ask what he means by the word 'correct' in this context. Does he mean 'correct' in the sense of being right as against wrong (or mistaken), or in the sense that some prescribed procedure has been properly followed by the agent? Note that neither sense of 'correct' entails the other. A person may be correct in the sense of being right virtually without having implemented procedures. And, conversely, a person may employ perfectly reasonable procedures and still not be right. The only direct explication of his meaning of 'correct' is to be found in a footnote. Given its central importance to his definition, close attention should be paid to it.

> This basic notion was suggested by B. Othenel Smith ('The improvement of critical thinking', *Progressive Education, xxx, p. 5)*: 'Now if we set about to find out what ... [a] statement means and to determine whether to accept or reject it, we would be engaged in thinking which, for lack of a better term, we shall call critical thinking.' Since Smith's definition does not use any word like 'correct', his notion is slightly different.
>   Smith's concept of *critical thinking* permits us to speak of 'good critical thinking' and 'poor critical thinking' without redundance or contradiction. Though this is an accepted manner of speaking, the predominant manner of speaking presumably builds the notion of correct thinking into the notion of critical thinking.[6]

On this latter point I would argue that the 'predominant manner of speaking' does not build correctness into the meaning of critical thinking: only logicians and philosophers trying to formalize things would make such a requirement. But this requirement does indicate the direction in which, presumably, Ennis is trying to go. Much more important, though, is that from a logical point of view. Smith's notion of critical thinking is not 'slightly different' from Ennis's but radically different, the major difference being twofold: first Smith's definition would permit, but Ennis's does not, degrees of critical thinking (that is, it is a relative notion for Smith); second, for Ennis the relationship between critical thinking and being correct is analytic, whereas for Smith it is not.

Having looked at Ennis's explication of his definition, 'the correct assessing of statements', we can return to our original question: what does he mean by 'correct'? Does he mean being right? Or does he mean that certain procedures are (correctly) followed? Given the following considerations:

1 that Ennis wants to distinguish his notion of critical thinking from Smith's (which permits degrees) by adding the word 'correct' instead of perhaps words like 'plausible', 'reasonable', or 'sensible';
2 that Ennis rules out the phrases 'good critical thinking', and 'bad critical thinking' as 'redundant' and 'contradictory' respectively.
3 that Ennis criticizes Dewey for not 'providing a logical criterion for the solution of a problem';

It seems that by the word 'correct' Ennis must mean 'being right' in the sense of not being mistaken or of possessing the truth. That is, Ennis is advancing a formal or absolute notion of critical thinking that permits of neither degrees nor mistakes. If he did not mean this, he would (or should) have no objection to Smith's definition. Clearly, then, Ennis's view of critical thinking is just wrong – not only wrong as a descriptive analysis, but ill-advised or wrong-headed as a prescription as well.

That Ennis's view is wrong as a descriptive analysis of the concept can be seen from several perspectives. First, as already mentioned, a person may be right about a statement, in the sense of possessing the truth, for reasons that have little or nothing to do with critical thinking. He may have merely absorbed his opinion as part of a peer group's attitude, for example, or he may have read and believed it, without question, in a popular magazine.

Moreover, our language does not merely permit us to talk about degrees of critical thinking, as Smith's definition suggests, but actually demands it. This is because thinking is a task, which may or may not result in the achievement of its desired end. Some efforts in thinking approximate success more closely than others; thus we can and do talk about 'good critical thinking', as Smith suggests, and we mean by this that some efforts are more intelligent, astute or perceptive than others. To follow Ennis and regard the connection between critical thinking and being correct as analytic would have the odd consequence of not being able to speak coherently about efforts to think critically. One would either have thought critically or not, depending on whether one is correct in the sense of right. But this is like using 'winning' in place of 'playing', which does a disservice to language and to the way in which we normally think about games.

In particular, what seems to have gone wrong in Ennis's analysis is that he (temporarily?) failed to recognize that what makes some bit of thinking critical is a function not of the result but of the way in which a particular result is pursued. Just as rationality is a function not of what is believed but of the way in which a belief is arrived at, so too with critical thinking. The precise result of a given assessment of statements is quite beside the point; to add the requirement of being correct is even more irrelevant.

Perhaps more important, however, there are also serious epistemic problems with Ennis's analysis of critical thinking as the correct assessment of statements. First, from a theoretical point of view, there is no independent way of determining when someone has correctly assessed a statement. If nothing else, the history of philosophy and the history of science have taught us to tread lightly through this field. Indeed, we continue to have cause to question the very criteria we use for knowledge, and statements as well as observations are just part of this fallibility. More concretely, however, even in those practical contexts in which critical thinking is urgently needed, we are frequently forced to choose between 'expert' testimonies that conflict with one another. Experts frequently disagree. Are we to say in such cases that no party has used critical thinking? Ennis's analysis of critical thinking cannot accommodate these common occurrences because of his overly stringent requirements of correctness. Yet these are precisely the cases in which critical thinking is most often needed. And these are also the cases in which our language, fortunately, permits talk about degrees of critical thinking.

My objections to Ennis's analysis of critical thinking also serve as objections to any suggestion that we should prescribe or stipulate such a meaning for the phrase 'critical thinking'. From a theoretical point of view, it would be self-defeating because we can seldom know when we have made a correct assessment of statements; and this deficiency is not without serious consequences for research into and the teaching of critical thinking. But perhaps more important from a linguistic and conceptual point of view, the concept of critical thinking would lose much of the subtlety and needed flexibility that it now possesses.

Let us assume, despite the textual evidence already cited, that Ennis means that one must be correct not in the sense of right, but rather in the sense that one goes through certain prescribed procedures in thinking. (One could in fact interpret Ennis's twelve 'aspects' and three 'dimensional criteria' as attempts to provide just such prescribed procedures.) However, setting aside the difficulties of squaring this interpretation with his discussion at the beginning, there are internal problems that render it equally unacceptable.

As Ennis says, his list of twelve 'aspects' of critical thinking do not really originate with him but are condensed from other works on logic and critical thinking that can be found in the literature. Ennis's list is as follows:

1   grasping the meaning of a statement;
2   judging whether there is ambiguity in a line of reasoning;
3   judging whether certain statements contradict each other;
4   judging whether a conclusion follows necessarily;
5   judging whether a statement is specific enough;
6   judging whether a statement is actually the application of a certain principle;
7   judging whether an observation statement is

       reliable;
   8   judging whether an inductive conclusion is
       warranted;
   9   judging whether the problem has been identified;
   10 judging whether something is an assumption;
   11 judging whether a definition is adequate;
   12 judging whether a statement made by an alleged
       authority is acceptable.

Like other authors on this topic, Ennis describes his twelve
'aspects' as 'pitfalls' which are to be avoided in the
'assessment of statements', that is, in areas where errors in
assessment can occur. In effect, such lists attempt to
itemize all the ways in which one could go wrong, or be
mistaken, in one's assessment of statements. However,
this approach to critical thinking has much in common with
a hypothetical attempt to list all the ways in which people
should be careful in order to avoid accidents of any kind, or
all the ways in which it is possible to lose a war or have a
soccer team come out at the bottom of a match. In all such
cases there is a more or less infinite number of ways in
which one could go wrong; therefore any such list is
doomed to failure.

     One might nonetheless defend such lists of 'pitfalls' on
the grounds that they often provide useful guidance or
helpful hints for avoiding common errors. But lists of
helpful hints do not provide a characterization of the
nature of the thing in question. (In chess one should learn
what checkmate means before accepting hints for
accomplishing or avoiding it.) In this case, since we are still
trying to determine what critical thinking is, we are hardly
in a position to judge the efficacy of helpful hints.

     However, a more important objection to interpreting
Ennis's meaning of 'correct' thinking via these twelve
'aspects' is to be found in his discussion of their
dimensional criteria. To that I shall now turn.

Ennis's dimensional simplification

It is quite clear that Ennis's most original contribution to the literature on critical thinking, and probably the most important, is his introduction to what he calls a 'dimensional simplification' of the concept. Previous discussions of critical thinking had listed various skills or 'aspects' that were thought to be part of the repertoire of critical thinking. But Ennis's discussion of the dimensions of critical thinking shows that the earlier 'skills' approach was far too simplistic, and that each skill has in fact other features (or 'dimensions') that are required for their rational application. In effect, he argues that the critical thinker should not only possess certain skills, but must also employ them in constant conjunction with other 'dimensional' considerations. It is not enough to have skills, he points out; one must also know when and how much to use them in appropriate circumstances.

Ennis begins his discussion of these dimensions by asserting: 'There are three basic analytically distinguishable dimensions of the proposed concept of critical thinking: a logical dimension, a criterial dimension, and a pragmatic dimension.'[7] Beyond the twelve 'aspects', then, these dimensions attempt to describe the relevant contextual considerations within which critical skills must operate and without which our understanding of the concept of critical thinking is incomplete.

Ennis describes the logical dimension thus:

> The *logical dimension*, roughly speaking, covers judging alleged relationships between meanings of words and statements. A person who is competent in this dimension knows what follows from a statement, or a group of statements, by virtue of their meaning. He particularly knows how to use the logical operators, 'all', 'some', 'none', 'not', 'if … then', 'or', 'unless', etc. He knows what it is for something to be a member of a class of things. Furthermore he knows the meaning of the basic terms in the field in which the statement under consideration is made.[8]

Ennis also has two footnotes that elaborate on this dimension, which make it clear that he means that both syntactic and semantic considerations constitute 'knowing the meaning of a term or statement', and that for him, 'understanding the meaning of a statement' entails 'knowing the implications of the statement'.

Somewhat less precisely, Ennis describes the criterial dimension as follows:

> The *criterial dimension* covers knowledge of the criteria for judging statements (soon to be described), except for the logical criteria, which are covered by the logical dimension.

Actually, Ennis fails to make good on his promise to describe this dimension further, but we can ascertain his meaning of this dimension from his discussion of 'aspect 7', 'judging whether an observation statement is reliable'. He says:

> An observation statement is a specific description. Over the years, those fields most concerned with accuracy of observation have built up a set of rules for judging the reliability of observation statements. These rules give a *criterial* dimension to this aspect of critical thinking.[9]

This dimension simply points out that various discipline-related subjects have established their own criteria for judging the accuracy and reliability of its statements.

Last, Ennis describes the pragmatic dimension as follows:

> The *pragmatic dimension* covers the impression of the background purpose of the judgement, and it covers the decision as to whether the statement is *good enough* for the purpose. Including this dimension does not constitute endorsement of the doctrine often attributed to pragmatism: 'A statement is true if it fulfils the purpose of the speaker.' But the inclusion of this dimension does constitute recognition of the legitimate function played by the background purpose in making decisions about the acceptability of statements. It does constitute recognition of the necessity for the balancing of factors preceding the judgment, 'This is enough evidence.' Furthermore, inclusion of this dimension requires the recognition that complete criteria cannot be established for critical thinking. An element of intelligent judgement is usually required in addition to applying criteria and knowing the meaning.[10]

This dimension points out that the relative importance of the consequences of being right or wrong must come into play in our assessment of statements; that is, judgements about having enough evidence must be related to the practical consequences.

It is worth noting here that the pragmatic dimension reveals dramatically how arbitrary is Ennis's decision to restrict critical thinking to the 'assessment of statements' and not to include decisions as well. Clearly, for example, a military general pondering the attack of a fortified hill is concerned primarily with assessing not the utterance 'Attack that hill', but the very real consequences of his actually deciding to attack the hill. Critical thinking is here required for assessing the decision, as such, and not for assessing a statement.

The following schema represents a simplified summary of Ennis's dimensional analysis:

1 *Logical dimension:* judging the alleged relations between terms, statements and sets of statements. This includes knowing the meanings of the terms and statements and their implications.
2 *Criterial dimension:* covers knowledge of the standards and subject-related criteria for judging statements, for example, statistical judgements in the social sciences.
3 *Pragmatic dimension:* judging, in context, when one has 'enough' evidence in the light of the statement's purpose and practical consequences.

I think it fair to say that these dimensions do represent a genuine contribution to the literature on critical thinking. For one thing, they highlight the fact that critical thinking is not merely the knee-jerk application of various skills, nor the simple application of formal logic and the detection of fallacies. They bring to the analysis of critical thinking, for the first time, the importance of the *setting* in which a judgement is made, its practical consequences and its relation to specific knowledge and information. I think Ennis is absolutely right in identifying that these considerations as integral parts of critical thinking. It is a pity that research, courses and programmes in critical thinking that virtually ignore these crucial dimensions persist. The so-called 'informal logic' approach is perhaps the worst offender in this regard.

But it is these dimensions, valid as they are, that are responsible for the failure of Ennis's definition and the deficiencies of his prescriptions. In the first place, contrary to the prevailing view, the criterial dimension clearly links specialized (field-dependent) knowledge with the concept of critical thinking itself. Indeed, the criterial dimension is defined in terms of various standards and subject-related criteria for judging statements in special fields. There are, however, innumerable fields of human knowledge, ranging from photography to astrophysics, and each has its own information, skills and standards of assessment. The criterial dimension of critical thinking precludes the *a priori* isolation or abstraction of any special set of particular skills to characterize it. Thus Ennis's twelve 'aspects' – which, incidentally, he often calls 'skills' – cannot contain the inherent diversity of critical thinking: they cannot, therefore, define it. Precisely what ingredients actually constitute the 'correct assessment of statements' cannot in general be foretold. His dimensional analysis, which properly includes different standards of assessment, undermines his definition of critical thinking.

Somewhat less obviously but just as certainly, the logical dimension has similar consequences, which further undermine the definition and proposals. We may recall that Ennis defines this dimension in terms of both the semantic and the syntactic dimensions of logic. That is, not only must a person be able to judge the alleged relations between words and statements, but he must also understand the meaning of the statements. And for Ennis 'understanding the meaning of a statement' entails 'knowing the logical implications of the statement' as well. But here again the logical dimension includes the sophisticated understanding of, and expertise in, specialized fields of knowledge. For the intelligent novice in an area it might represent quite an achievement merely to understand the simple meaning of a statement, but nothing short of an arduous initiation into the field would permit him to see all of its 'logical implications' as well. Ennis's logical dimension, however, includes this sophisticated understanding. Thus the logical dimension encompasses the highest levels of understanding in the various fields of knowledge. A logical consequence of this, as in the case of the criterial dimension, is that the so-called 'critical thinking skills' cannot be distinguished from intellectual knowledge and skills in general. These latter are part and parcel of the concept of critical thinking. Again, therefore, the adequacy of Ennis's twelve 'aspects' (or 'skills') is called into question.

Last, and perhaps most obvious, Ennis's pragmatic dimension has the most devastating effects on any attempt to define critical thinking in terms of finite 'aspects' or 'skills', including Ennis's own list of these. The pragmatic dimension, remember, involves judging when one has enough evidence for something, the proper amount of evidence being a function of the purpose for which it was offered, and the severity of the consequences if wrong. In effect, the pragmatic dimension places critical thinking squarely in the arena of an infinity of possible kinds of judgements with an infinite number of possible consequences. This is because the purpose and contexts of assertions vary independently and unpredictably. Indeed, recognition of this fact prompted Ennis, in his discussion of the pragmatic dimension, to make the following admission.

> Furthermore, inclusion of this dimension requires the recognition that complete criteria cannot be established for critical thinking. An element of intelligent judgement is usually required in addition to applying criteria and knowing the meaning.[11]

This is an extremely telling admission because it effectively acknowledges that this dimension confers on critical thinking more complexity than the attempted definition could possibly absorb. I would go further and suggest that this same limitation applies equally to the other two dimensions as well. What is surprising, however, is that Ennis makes this admission about the pragmatic dimension, yet does not appear to notice the destructive implications it has for his own case. He is saying, in effect, that if the pragmatic dimension is taken into proper consideration, the 'correct assessment of statements' cannot be specified. Had he carried his reasoning further, he would have seen that this is also why the 'correct assessment of statements' does not define critical thinking.

All three of Ennis's dimensions reveal that critical thinking is integrally connected with specific knowledge and information, not to mention contingent contexts, and cannot for this reason be divorced from them. This is why I believe any effort to characterize, let alone define, critical thinking in terms of some finite number of teachable skills is destined to failure,[12] and why all such lists of so-called 'skills', upon analysis, typically degenerate into collections of near-tautologies or the most obvious kind of vacuous advice (for example, 'Select data that support your conclusion'; 'Do not contradict yourself'). None of this is particularly insightful or helpful.

Ennis's twelve 'aspects'

Ennis's list of twelve 'aspects' of critical thinking is perhaps more sensible than most such lists because he tries to delineate specific criteria for applying them. But because he tries to be explicit in this regard, sometimes the inadequacies of the aspects show through clearly. For example, in discussing the first aspect on his list, 'grasping the meaning of a statement', Ennis is constrained to impose arbitrary and unreasonable limits for the sake of keeping it manageable, perhaps for teachers and researchers. After stating that a person 'should know what, if anything, a statement would imply in a situation and what would imply it', he immediately imposes the following qualification:

> The things to be known should, of course, not be expected to be more sophisticated than the statement in question, nor should they be expected to include things that are distantly removed.[13]

But not only does this qualification contradict his characterization of the logical dimension, which was presented without qualifications, but this is an obvious Procrustean treatment of the phenomena to fit his preconceived idea of the task. The world of events, situations, conversations and assertions just happens to be such that they are frequently more complicated or sophisticated than they might seem at first flush or than we might like. But we cannot arbitrarily assert that 'the knowledge presupposed by a statement cannot be more sophisticated than the statement itself', without seriously distorting the realities of the way the world is. However, this type of qualification is typically needed to fit critical thinking into a bed of finite skills that are alleged to characterize it.

A more obvious and undoubtedly more serious limitation imposed on Ennis's list, and thence on critical thinking itself, is the elimination of value judgements. Ennis says of these:

> Although the root notion calls for its inclusion, the judging of value statements is deliberately excluded from the above list. This exclusion admittedly weakens the attractiveness of the presented concept, but makes it more manageable. So long as we remember that this exclusion has occurred, we should not be confused by the truncated concept. Perhaps this gap can at some future time be at least partially filled.[14]

This looks like the innocent use of author's licence to restrict discussion for the sake of convenience. And it also implies that this 'gap' might be treated 'at some future time'. In truth, however, this omission is anything but an innocent or benign use of author's licence. Instead, it is typical of the qualifications that are required to make the ailment fit the prearranged treatments. That it is not innocent in this case can be seen from Ennis's later remark (towards the end of the paper) about the substantive and strategic effects of excluding value statements from critical thinking:

> This exclusion itself, by the way, exemplifies the choice of one concept over another. In order that prediction and control of students' behavior be facilitated, an unwieldy area (evaluating value statements) has been eliminated from the concept, *critical thinking*.[15]

Clearly, this is not an innocent restriction imposed by a

philosopher seeking truth about the nature of critical thinking. Rather, it is that of an engineer suggesting a way in which to shave an over-sized peg to fit a small hole: you first change the shape or distort the peg.

Nor is the exlusion of value judgements benign. On the contrary, it strikes the Achilles' heel of the 'skills' approach to critical thinking in general. In Ennis's case the severe limitations that result from the exclusion of value judgements reveal themselves throughout his discussion of the twelve 'aspects'. For example, in his discussion of the aspect 'judging whether the problem has been identified', Ennis is forced to beg off the problem:

> Judging that a valuable goal has been selected. Here is such a problem: 'Our problem in Culver City is to increase respect for law and order.' Insofar as that is a statement of an end rather than a means, the judgement that it is an adequate identification of a problem is a value judgement. For reasons indicated earlier [that these are 'unwieldy'], this type of judging, though important, is excluded from this concept of *critical thinking.*[16]

A further, more serious implication of this is, of course, that ends, as such, can never be the subject of critical thinking because they involve value judgements. But, clearly, critical thinking is required in the discussion of ends at least as much as it is required for the assessment of means. As in the present case, however, Ennis's 'truncated concept' of critical thinking is not merely a benign deletion of something relatively unimportant, but a severe limitation prohibiting the use of critical thinking from the most straightforward cases requiring it. This same limitation raises its head in his discussion of several other 'aspects' as well.

However, the most serious effect of the exclusion of value judgements from the domain of critical thinking is that it unwittingly excludes the pragmatic dimension from critical thinking. The pragmatic dimension requires balancing the amount of evidence required (for a judgement) against the consequences of being wrong. That is, the determination of how much evidence is enough is a direct function of how important it is that a statement be right or wrong. But importance can be assessed only in terms of the relative value placed on things by a person or group of persons. Thus the pragmatic dimension of critical thinking cannot be satisfied until one comes to grips with the value system involved in the judgement. A person's values are an integral feature of rational judgement, and the pragmatic dimension properly serves to underline this fact. Thus it is inconsistent, or at least self-defeating, to affirm the necessity of the pragmatic dimension for critical thinking on the one hand, and to exclude value judgements from its analysis on the other.

Critical thinking is shot through with value judgements on almost every level; the pragmatic dimension assures this. Failure to appreciate this has the unfortunate result that Ennis's conception is inapplicable in the most common of circumstances and must run foul of its own dimensional parameters. Thus the exclusion of value judgements can be considered a benign restriction (or limitation) from the point of view of neither critical thinking in general nor Ennis's analysis in particular.

One final point to be made about Ennis's discussion of critical thinking concerns his view that the twelve 'aspects' actually describe 'skills' or 'abilities'. Towards the end of his paper, for example, he switches from talking about 'twelve aspects of critical thinking' to 'twelve abilities'. This kind of switch is common in discussions of critical thinking. Grammatically, in fact, the change in usage seems to work just as well. However, it is wise in this instance to heed Gilbert Ryle's sage observation that grammatical sense can often lead to ontological confusion. Aside from our grammatical licence to speak in this way, Ennis provides no justification whatever for regarding his 'aspects' as generalized 'abilities'. Indeed, talk of generalized abilities, such as 'creative ability', 'reasoning ability', 'comprehension skills' and so on, has become ingrained in the ever-growing lexicon of educational jargon. Perhaps this stems from the temptation to reify the sort of items listed in B. S. Bloom's taxonomy; I am not sure. But it is seldom recognized that Bloom's whole edifice is constructed on the assumption that there are generalized abilities that transfer across logical boundaries.[17] In this particular case the phrase 'critical thinking ability', as it might be used in the sentence 'Everet has critical thinking ability', masks a similar assumption. This assumption in association with critical thinking, however, is implausible.

Consider, for example, the way in which we use such words as 'speed', 'effectiveness' and 'constructiveness'. In a specific context it might make grammatical sense to say, 'Everet has speed' or 'Alice is very effective', but we do not mean to convey the idea that speed or effectiveness are generalized skills that are deployed in everything which Everet or Alice might do. We recognize, tacitly or explicitly, that a person who has speed or is effective in one activity may not possess this characteristic in other activities; and, more important, we recognize that the specific ingredients for having speed or being effective are as varied as the different activities that can be pursued. In short, we recognize that speed and effectiveness are not generalized abilities, even though we can grammatically speak of them in this way.

Similarly, in specific contexts it makes sense to talk about 'critical thinking ability'. We might say, 'Everet is a critical historian' or 'Alice pursues sociology very critically', and these statements make perfectly good sense. But in saying these things we would not mean to imply that Everet or Alice possesses some generalized ability that would equally well apply to other activities because again we tacitly recognize that, like speed, effectiveness and constructiveness, critical thinking is not a generalized ability. Moreover, the discussion above of Ennis's three dimensions (the logical, the criterial and the pragmatic) shows precisely why critical thinking is not, in fact, a generalized ability: it is because critical thinking is linked conceptually with particular activities and special fields of knowledge. The reasons that prohibit us from isolating critical thinking from special fields and particular activities are the same reasons as those that make it impossible to conceive of critical thinking as a generalized skill.

More recently, Professor Ennis has expanded his

interest in critical thinking *per se* and is now working on rationality as a whole. In a recent paper entitled 'Notes for "A conception of rational thinking"'[18] Ennis again presents a long list of the 'characteristics of rational thinkers'. What is particularly noteworthy about this latest work is that seventeen years after the publication of the *Harvard Educational Review* paper, Ennis continues to make the same assumptions and to employ the same strategy for the analysis of rationality as he did with critical thinking. Predictably, therefore, this latest effort suffers from the same deficiencies as his analysis of critical thinking. This suggests, among other things, that we have not come very far in these past two decades. Until we free ourselves from the traps of our own jargon and recognize that terms like 'critical thinking' and 'rationality' do not denote generalized skills, we are not likely to increase this rate of progress.

Edward D'Angelo's concept of critical thinking

Edward D'Angelo's book *The Teaching of Critical thinking*[19] has several features that make it of some interest here. Far more thoroughly than most authors of books with a similar purpose, D'Angelo first attempts to probe the meaning of the concept of critical thinking in order to justify his pedogogical proposals. Writing nine years after the publication of Ennis's paper, D'Angelo purports to reject Ennis's definition of critical thinking. However, it is interesting to note the extent to which he has absorbed Ennis's basic approach and has made the same fundamental assumptions, thus perpetuating what has come to be the received view about critical thinking.

D'Angelo rejects Ennis's definition of critical thinking because it

> assumes there is always a correct or incorrect way of assessing statements. But there are disagreements where it is difficult to judge whether a correct assessment of a statement has been made. One disputant may contend there is adequate evidence to verify a particular belief, whereas another disputant may deny it. There are many borderline cases in which it is difficult

to determine who has correctly assessed a particular statement. The history of ethical disagreement also shows that it is sometimes impossible to determine who has correctly assessed an argument.[20]

But this argument does not show that there is not a correct way to assess statements, because all arguments, including D'Angelo's own, presuppose that there is a correct way; it merely shows that it is often difficult to determine which assessment is correct. The flaw in Ennis's phrase 'correct assessment of statements' is not that statements do not have correct assessments, nor that correctness is difficult to determine, but that being correct is deemed a possible consequence of critical thinking and not a description of the process itself.

Nevertheless, having officially rejected Ennis's definition, D'Angelo submits his own:

> Critical thinking is the process of evaluating statements, arguments, and experiences. An operational definition of critical thinking would consist of all the attitudes and skills used in the evaluating process.[21]

Aside from deleting the word 'correct' and including 'experiences', D'Angelo's definition is not markedly different from Ennis's. The inclusion of 'experiences' is potentially a significant difference because it could include non-propositional knowledge as well; however, D'Angelo does nothing whatever to develop this potential, but instead pursues the so-called 'evaluational skills' of statements with even more vigour than Ennis. His addition of 'experiences' is therefore spurious, and an opportunity to shed some new light on the concept has been missed.

The most noticeable addition to Ennis's analysis of critical thinking is that D'Angelo extends Ennis's list of twelve 'aspects' (or 'skills') to fifty 'skills' and ten 'attitudes'. It never seems to occur to him that such a long list (which could be interminable) might contain the seeds of a mistaken procedure. But D'Angelo perseveres with his list of 'skills'; like Ennis, be begins with 'determining the meaning of a statement' and provides an expository paragraph for each 'skill'. D'Angelo includes in his list all the items that Ennis has, plus the 'informal fallacies' and a few other 'skills' of his own reckoning, for example: 'the analysis of clichés', 'avoiding mistaking figurative language for literal language', 'distinguishing a fact from an opinion', 'judging common sense', 'the analysis of emotional language' and the like.[22] But under the new headings the list contains advice that has been available since Aristotle's *Rhetoric* and Quintilian's *Oratorium*.

To the list of skills D'Angelo adds 'the following attitudes which are necessary conditions for the development of critical thinking':

1   intellectual curiosity;
2   objectivity;
3   open-mindedness;
4   flexibility;
5   intellectual scepticism;
6   intellectual honesty;
7   being systematic;
8   persistence;
9   decisiveness;
10 respect for other viewpoints.[23]

While 'intellectual curiosity' and 'being systematic' can clearly be worthy traits in many contexts, I see no grounds for asserting that they are 'necessary conditions' for critical thinking. More troublesome for the fledgling student, however, would be the attempt to manifest 'open-mindedness', 'flexibility' and 'decisiveness' simultaneously. D'Angelo describes decisiveness as the capacity to

> reach certain conclusions when the evidence warrants it. To avoid unnecessarily drawn-out arguments, snap judgements, and delaying reaching decisions until all the necessary information is obtained.

And he describes as flexibility the willingness to

> change one's beliefs or methods of inquiry. Avoiding steadfastness of belief, dogmatic attitude, and rigidity. A realization that we do not know all the answers.[24]

As 'necessary conditions' of critical thinking, both of these requirements must be satisfied in any given case. But the satisfaction of one of these would simultaneously inhibit the other. If they are not formally contradictory, they are at least pragmatically impossible to satisfy at the same time. In any case, I see more confusion than elucidation resulting from insistence on their common necessity. Instead I think we should recognize that these attitudes can indeed be conducive to critical thinking at times but are not 'necessary conditions' of it. One item that D'Angelo omits from his list is the need to guard against the use of platitudes when analysis is required.

By far the most serious shortcoming of D'Angelo's analysis, however, is his persistent attempt to remove knowledge of facts and information from the domain of critical thinking. Even more than Ennis, who at least admits the necessity of facts through his 'dimensions', D'Angelo attempts to define critical thinking solely in terms of his 'skills' and 'attitudes'. In a sense, D'Angelo takes the general thrust of Ennis's paper further than a careful reading would allow. If it were literally true that a person could possess a skill without knowledge and information, then we could say such things as 'Everet has skill but in nothing in particular', which is absurd. The first evidence of D'Angelo's attempted purification of critical thinking by removing knowledge of facts appears on the first pages of the book:

> A knowledge of the subject area in which thinking occurs is often a necessary condition for the development of critical thinking. For example, certain knowledge is needed to determine whether a particular statement is a fact or an opinion. However, specific knowledge in a particular area is not always necessary in order to apply critical thinking skills
> . . . .
> The factors that seem to occur in all cases of critical thinking are certain attitudes and a knowledge and application of certain thinking skills.[25]

However, D'Angelo's use of the phrase 'often a necessary condition' is curious. Either something is a necessary condition for something or it is not, and if it is, then it is always so and not merely 'often' or sometimes. This is a dubious attempt to remove the necessity for knowledge and information from critical thinking by subverting the notion of a necessary condition. (Admittedly, D'Angelo's failure so to remove it actually saves him from himself, as it were, because his success would issue in the absurdity alluded to above.)

Normally I should not like to make too much of D'Angelo's misuse of the phrase 'necessary conditions', since in some circumstances it could represent a mere slip of the pen. But this confusion is far too pervasive throughout his book, and too much confusion is thereby generated, to let it pass. In several places, for example, D'Angelo dismisses the suggestions of other authors on the grounds that such-and-such a skill cannot be part of critical thinking because it is 'not always necessary in evaluation'. Are we to infer, then, that all of D'Angelo's fifty 'skills' and ten 'attitudes' are jointly manifest in each act of critical thinking? If so, then his view is clearly wrong, since at most only a few could be manifest; if not, then his skills are no different from these others, since, taken singularly, his too are only 'sometimes necessary'. What D'Angelo consistently does in these discussions, in fact, is to equivocate about the meaning of 'necessary' in order to dispose of competing suggestions by other authors. Presumably, D'Angelo is trying to maintain that his fifty 'skills' and ten 'attitudes' constitute logically 'necessary conditions' of critical thinking, whereas other skills, such as 'problem-solving abilities', 'interpretation skills' and so on, are only contingently necessary. Thus he dismisses each of these latter skills (which have been suggested by other authors) by pointing out that it is 'not always necessary, therefore it cannot form part of the definition of critical thinking'. But he fails to apply the same criterion to his own list of skills, which are, similarly, not always necessary, depending on the problem.

A typical example of how D'Angelo rejects suggested skills and procedures that are not part of his own (preferred) list can be clearly seen in his rejection of problem solving.

What is the relation of critical thinking to problem solving? Although there are various formulations of the procedures of problem solving, Dewey's concept of problem solving is most widely used by teachers. It consists of the following steps: (1) 'a felt difficulty', (2) stating the nature of the problem, (3) gathering data, (4) developing hypotheses, (5) reasoning about the consequences of hypotheses, and (6) testing these hypotheses. It would be inaccurate to define critical thinking in terms of problem solving. Critical thinking consists of more skills than are used in the problem-solving approach, and some of these steps include intuitive and creative elements that do not involve any evaluation or justification. All we can say is that some critical thinking skills are used in the problem solving approach.[26]

It might be true that 'critical thinking consists of more skills than are used in the problem-solving approach', but that is not the point. The point is that D'Angelo provides no reason for rejecting 'problem solving' simply because it is only a part of critical thinking. The items in his own list after all are similarly, at best, only a part of critical thinking. D'Angelo uses an *a priori* selection criterion that has never been justified.

D'Angelo's rejection of R. Karlin's suggestion that interpretive reading skills are an important part of critical thinking is not only arbitrary but also contradictory to some basic tenants of his own position in the process:

Karlin contends that critical reading can be developed in the classroom by asking students to compare and evaluate pictures, judge whether a story is plausible, seek confirmation of certain beliefs by examining source materials, select biased and distorted statements, and determine the facts and opinions in books and periodicals. This is the evaluative aspect of his concept of critical reading. Karlin also suggests that students seek meanings and messages of literary works, compare characters in a story to children they know, and discuss events relative to their own standards. These activities do not entail the use of critical thinking skills. When a student claims that the message of Antoine de Saint Exupéry's *The Little Prince* is the importance of being concerned about others, there is no indication from this response that an evaluation has taken place. The stated message of this book may have been derived from a synopsis or it may be an intuitive belief.[27]

This last objection, while possibly true, is clearly reaching for straws and pressing logical possibilities beyond credulity. After all, this type of objection could be levelled at any human utterance whatever and, if pressed consistently, would lead to absolute solipsism. In the end everyone, including D'Angelo, must assume that a person's utterances and behaviour are the most direct evidence of what he is thinking or has thought.

The most telling claim in D'Angelo's rejection of Karlin, however, is that all the aforementioned interpretive skills 'do not entail the use of critical thinking skills'. Presumably, what D'Angelo is trying to say is that interpretation by itself does not constitute critical thinking. What he does not seem to recognize, however, is that interpretation is a logically necessary condition for critical thinking. The argument for this, of course, would be, first, that critical thinking entails evaluation (this is D'Angelo's major claim and part of his definition) and, second, that evaluation entails interpretation (one could not be said to be 'evaluating' if one did not understand the basic material or data of the evaluation); therefore (by hypothetical syllogism) critical thinking entails interpretation. Thus interpretation is a necessary condition of critical thinking. But it is all the more surprising that D'Angelo does not seem to recognize this relation because his denial of it, *contra* Karlin, directly contradicts several of his own designated skills, which, he says, help to define critical thinking. In his list of fifty skills, for example, we find: 'determining the meaning of a statement', 'the analysis of emotional language', 'interpreting words with regard to context', 'avoiding mistaking figurative language for literal language' and so on, all of which are 'interpretive' skills *par excellence*. Thus, on pain of inconsistency, he has no grounds whatever for rejecting what seems to me a perfectly sensible suggestion by Karlin. I think this is a clear example of the kind of myopia that can take hold when one becomes overly enámoured of a definition. In this case, moreover, an 'outsider' from reading is trespassing into the traditional grounds of philosophy and informal logic. I have come to expect resistance, but not at such a high price.

Once it is clearly seen – Ennis saw this partially and D'Angelo not at all – that specific content, knowledge and information cannot be coherently demarcated from critical thinking, then it will be acknowledged that it is the domain not of any particular discipline but of all. Theoretical attempts to isolate the concept are forced to emasculate the concept almost beyond recognition. It is time that the prevailing view recognized that critical thinking is more complex than originally envisaged.

NOTES

1. I. A. Snook, 'Teaching pupils to think', *Studies in Philosophy and Education*, vol. 8, no. 3 (Winter, 1974), pp. 154–5.
2. 'A concept of critical thinking', *Harvard Educational Review*, vol. 32, no. 1 (Winter 1962), pp. 81–111. In the remainder of this chapter I shall simply use the initials HER to refer to this paper.
3. *HER*, p. 83.
4. The ambiguous intent, or at least outcome, of Ennis's paper is also manifest in the differing interpretations of it offered by subsequent writers. For example, Bryce B. Hudgins, *Learning and Thinking* (Itasca, Ill.: F. E. Peacock, 1978), interprets Ennis as presenting a descriptive definition of what critical thinking is, whereas Edward D'Angelo, *The Teaching of Critical Thinking* (Amsterdam: B. R. Grüner, 1971) sees Ennis as presenting a normative definiton for the purpose of delineating teachable skills.
5. *HER*, p. 82.
6. *HER*, p. 83f.
7. *HER*, p. 84.
8. *HER*, pp. 84–5.
9. *HER*, p. 90. As my discussion of these dimensions will show later, it is significant that Ennis should somehow forget or otherwise fail to elaborate on this dimension in particular.
10. *HER*, p. 85.
11. *ibid.*
12. Even as a so-called 'range definition', these dimensions preclude his twelve 'aspects' from 'covering the same indefinite territory' that is required.
13. *HER*, p. 86.
14. *HER*, p. 84.
15. *HER*, p. 102.
16. *HER*, p. 97.

17. This point about Bloom's taxonomy has also been made by Robin Barrow in *Common Sense and the Curriculum* (London: George Allen and Unwin, 1976), p. 37.
18. Presented as the Presidential Address to the Thirty-Fifth meeting of the Philosophy of Education Society, Toronto, 20 April 1979. The *Proceedings* are in press at the time of writing.
19. D'Angelo, *The Teaching of Critical Thinking*.
20. *ibid.*, p. 7.
21. *ibid.*, p. 7.
22. *ibid.*, pp. 9–15.
23. *ibid.*, pp. 7, 8.
24. *ibid.*
25. *ibid.*, pp. 1–2.
26. *ibid.*, p. 19.
27. *ibid.*, p. 30.

CHAPTER 4

Informal Logic and Critical Thinking

During the past twenty-five years universities in Britain and North America have commonly offered courses under such titles as 'Introduction to Logic', 'Critical Thinking' or 'Critical Reasoning'. Such courses are typically justified by the claim that they improve students' critical thinking ability. Whatever the title may be, the content of such courses consists chiefly of informal logic. No one, as far as I am aware, has ever argued that the terms 'critical thinking' and 'logic' are synonymous, yet practice has conflated the two.

However, the slightest reflection on the matter forces us to admit that there are (and have been) critical thinkers in this world who have never heard of informal logic. Conversely, there are students who have mastered the required exercises in informal logic texts yet in many other contexts would not qualify as critical thinkers. In short, informal logic and critical thinking are not the same thing. Nor is it clear that one implies the other. What is now required is a more careful look at the connections that are thought to exist between these endeavours. Some proponents of informal logic assume without argument that the two notions are linked logically in some way, perhaps by definition. Others recognize that the two notions are distinct but argue that there is an important contingent connection. Informal logic is thought to provide the basic skills, or tools, for becoming a critical thinker in wider contexts. Presumably, the connection is thought to be like that between five-finger exercises and piano concertos. Indeed, two ardent proponents of courses in informal logic have recently suggested that it is right and proper that 'informal logic is increasingly seen as the tool for the critical analysis of reasoning, and its raw material, *wherever* they occur.[1] Whether or not this claim is the simple over-statement that it appears to be depends to a large extent on what one means by informal logic. This term remains about as vague as it could be, despite the many informal logic texts that are published every year. The persistent vagueness of the phrase has permitted all sorts of claims for it to go unchallenged.

Text books on informal logic, including some of the better ones, such as W. W. Fernside's and W. B. Holther's *Fallacy: The Counterfeit of Argument*[2] and Michael Scriven's *Reasoning*,[3] generally begin with various promissory notes to the effect that mastery of the material will enable students to become more rational, will provide them with critical skills and will prevent them from being deceived by bad arguments.[4] However, they are usually too pre-occupied with getting on with the business of naming and describing fallacies to devote much space to explaining precisely what informal logic is supposed to be.

However, we may acquire a loose idea of what informal logic is by gleaning the contents of one of the texts on the subject. The books invariably contain lengthy discussions of various informal 'fallacies', some discussion of Aristotle's syllogisms and a few formal fallacies, and a discussion of vague and ambiguous language. This subject matter has constituted the common core of these texts for years. Indeed, their content differs very little from what the Greco-Roman and medieval traditions taught as rhetoric: the art of persuading and convincing. C. Perelman and L. Olbrechts-Tyteca have even published a lengthy treatise on this subject under the title *The New Rhetoric: A Treatise on Argumentation*.[5] A most refreshing aspect of this book is that while its authors are aware of the inability of formal logic, or the 'inductive–deductive' paradigm, to account for most real argument, they do not pretend to have found another logic ('informal logic') with which to replace it. Theirs is a more realistic undertaking, as the word 'rhetoric' in the title accurately suggests. Contemporary informal logicians, on the other hand, insist that there is more to informal logic than the study of rhetoric. But wherein lies the difference? What does informal logic offer that rhetoric does not? And how might informal logic improve critical thinking?

To answer these questions it is instructive to look at the answers recently provided by Ralph H. Johnson and J. Anthony Blair in their paper 'The recent development of informal logic'.[6] This paper is an attempt to exalt informal logic to the status of an autonomous discipline, though Johnson and Blair admit that they 'may be writing more a manifesto than a review'.

R. H. Johnson and J. A. Blair on informal logic

Informal logic and classical rhetoric have far more in common than proponents in either area like to admit. For example, both areas begin by distinguishing their enterprises from formal demonstration, which character-izes logic, geometry, mathematics and other formal sciences. In these latter areas, inferences are justified or prohibited by direct ·appeal to the formal rules. But informal logic and rhetoric do not have the advantage of formal rules (hence the term 'informal'), so that mistakes in reasoning and argument must be characterized by other, less precise means. The respective histories of rhetoric and informal logic reveal that both approaches to argument make use of so-called 'fallacies' to characterize errors in reasoning. The notion of a fallacy in these contexts cannot be applied with the same precision as an axiom or formal detachment rule and is best thought of as signifying merely a mistake (of some kind) in reasoning. C. L. Hamblin defines such 'errors' simply as 'arguments that *seem* valid but are not'.

One might be tempted to suggest that the difference between rhetoric and informal logic resides in their purpose or domain of application. But both are concerned with praxis – praxis, moreover, for the same domain. In particular, in origin and development rhetoric has tended to emphasize the study of the art of persuasion, deliberation and discussion as it is found in everyday discourse and oratory. It, like informal logic, has always included the study of the reasoning and persuasive power of moral, legal and political argument. Johnson and Blair, who want to distinguish logic from rhetoric, define informal logic as

> that area of logic (not yet fully canonized as a discipline) which attempts to formulate the principles and standards of logic which are necessary for the evaluation of ordinary argumentation. We take this to include not only the generation of procedures for appraising arguments but also the articulation of supporting theory.[7]

The introduction of the honorific word 'logic' into the first part of this definition serves more to confuse than to clarify because, clearly, the word does not carry its normal denotation here. Informal logic and rhetoric distinguish themselves from the demonstrative sciences by the absence of formal detachment rules, the hallmark of logical systems. Indeed, there is an important sense in which the phrase 'informal logic' is a contradiction in terms; if something is truly informal (that is, it has no detachment rules), then it is not logical in the normal sense of the word. The term 'logic', then, neither explains the meaning of informal logic nor distinguishes it from rhetoric.

It is in the second part of Johnson and Blair's definition of informal logic that we must look for its meaning. In particular, we must look to the claim that informal logic 'attempts to formulate the principles and standards of logic which are necessary for the evaluation of ordinary argumentation', and that this is to include 'procedures for appraising arguments' and also 'the articulation of supporting theory'.[8] Here perhaps we see the ambition of informal logic rather than its precise description, but this does much to distinguish informal logic from rhetoric because it is precisely this ambition (or aspirations) to formulate a comprehensive theory of argument that characterizes informal logic and distinguishes it from rhetoric. Historically, rhetoric has been content to name and describe discrete types of argument and fallacies piecemeal, whereas informal logic attempts to codify 'ordinary argumentation' into a general theory that 'formulates principles' and provides general 'standards of evaluation'. Aside from this, no other characteristic distinguishes informal logic from rhetoric. Indeed, it is the endeavour to formulate such theory that Johnson and Blair wish to 'canonize as a discipline'.

There is considerable evidence in Johnson's and Blair's paper to suggest that they view the principal difference between informal logic and rhetoric as residing in 'analysis and criticism', these latter being the domain of informal logic. But this alleged difference will not stand up to scrutiny. There is ample evidence that rhetoricians, particularly Perelman and Olbrechts-Tyteca, are as concerned about analysis and criticism as informal logicians. Indeed, the detailed descriptions of various fallacies and rhetorical techniques offered by rhetoricians often surpass the best work of informal logicians. What Johnson and Blair mean to say, perhaps, is that rhetoricians do not supply the kind of analysis and criticism that informal logicians desire: the kind that leads to general principles and the formulation of theory. Thus the real difference between rhetoric and informal logic resides in this desire (or aspiration) of informal logicians for a general theory of argument.

Before examining the extent to which informal logicians have succeeded in their attempts at formulating such a theory, it is worth considering the nature of the goal to which they aspire. Setting aside for the moment the precise meaning of 'ordinary argumentation' (a term about which informal logicians are particularly vague), we might ask what it would be like to have a general theory of ordinary argument or reasoning. For one thing, the theory would provide a set of rules or principles to which one could appeal in the evaluation of arguments. But if informal logicians were ever successful at developing all these rules and principles, they would then have a formal logic of ordinary argument or reasoning; that is, the desired theory would vitiate the informal dimension of their reasoning and render their enterprise a *bona fide* logic, which could then be taught as the formal logic of ordinary reasoning. But is a logic of ordinary reasoning even possible? Are there any grounds for thinking such a theory of argumentation could be constructed? At the moment it seems that there is little more than blind faith in the constant requests for principles or rules to justify inferences or to support charges of fallacy. There is the implicit assumption that for every bit of reasoning there must be some principle to justify it. And given that principles are by their nature general, the thinking seems to be that these general principles can be codified into a theory of reasoning – hence Johnson's and Blair's search for 'the generation of procedures' and 'supporting theory'. The most memorable propositions of other philosophers who thought that principles must underlie every inference and that a general theory of reasoning was possible are Spinoza's 'Geometrical method' and Descartes' *Rules for the Direction of the Mind.* But the history of philosophy has shown these methods to be deficient in two ways: first, intuitions are required that are not themselves grounded in principle and differ from person to person; second, the methods have very restricted domains of valid application.

This desire of informal logicians to develop a theory of argumentation rests on two articles of faith, both of which I believe to be unfounded. One is the view that if a piece of reasoning is justified, then its justification must reside in some further principle. But the mistake here is to confuse the notion of having a justification with that of the use of a general principle. Not all justified decisions (or judgements) employ general principles – at least, not the kind required for a theory. In addition to justified *sui generis* judgements, there are decisions and judgements that are justified by contingent events and circumstances. But, more important, there are justified decisions and judgements that rest simply on experience and can be supported in no other way. Indeed, it is arguable that most justified beliefs, decisions and judgements are of this kind.

The other article of faith underlying the search for a theory of argumentation is the implicit idea that a principle applied in one area of human experience must also apply in others; that is, if something is to be a *bona fide* principle of reason, then it must be generalizable. This line of reasoning assumes that being generalizable is, for all intents and purposes, equivalent to being repeatable. However, the assumption overlooks a crucial distinction, that between principles repeatable within a domain and those applying to several domains. Just as the rules of a particular game do not necessarily apply to other games, so certain principles of reason apply within some spheres of human experience but not in others. A principle of reason in business or law, for example, might be fallacious in science or ethics.[9] This is neither surprising nor profound, but it is a point that is continually obscured by informal logicians, and it may explain their optimism about the development of a general theory of argumentation.

In sum, there is at present little to distinguish informal logic from rhetoric save the attempt to generate a theory of ordinary argumentation by informal logicians. The above discussion – indeed, this entire essay – provides reasons for suspecting the feasibility of formulating such a theory because it rests on two highly questionable assumptions: first, that every justified piece of reasoning must be sanctioned by some general principle of reason, which is itself justifiable; second, that principles of reason apply across domains, regardless of subject matter.[10]

The bulk of Johnson's and Blair's paper reviews recent contributions and developments in informal logic and points out where more work is urgently needed. The authors suggest that research in the field falls into two distinguishable areas: the theory of fallacy and the theory of argumentation. I shall comment on each of these areas in turn for the purpose of assessing their progress.

The theory of fallacy

Perhaps I should say at the outset that my impression has been that the teaching and learning of informal fallacies has suffered from what I shall term the Charlie Brown Syndrome. This is encapsulated in a *Peanuts* cartoon, in which Lucy, sitting behind an official-looking orange crate (with umbrella) and a sign saying, 'Psychiatric Help – 5 cents', says to Charlie, 'For five cents, if you tell me what is bothering you today, I'll give you a name for it.' In much the same way, the teaching of informal logic appears to involve little more than providing names for obvious mistakes in reasoning. And just as in Charlie Brown's case, it is not clear that anything of value has been gained.

The teaching of informal fallacies has usually consisted in describing and naming most well-known fallacies, such as those of language (for example, ambiguity, equivocation and so on), attempts to beg questions, appeals to the emotions, attacks on character or circumstance, irrelevant reasons or false causes, and several others of more recent vintage, such as 'strawman' and 'slippery slope'. Students are taught to recognize these fallacies by doing various exercises and then picking them out of newspaper editorials, political speeches, advertisements and other popular sources. The initial exercises are usually obvious cases of fallacy, since they have been constructed for textbook purposes. However, upon moving from the simple textbook examples to more complex, real-life examples, serious problems ensue for both teacher and students. The source of these problems is always the same: the absence of definitive criteria for distinguishing fallacious from non-fallacious propositions. Moreover, arguments are sometimes weak for reasons that have little or nothing to do with fallacy, yet these reasons are not clearly distinguished from ·*bona fide* fallacies. Exasperation with these perennial problems has forced many an informal logic teacher simply to drop the fallacies altogether.

These same problems, however, have incited proponents of the fallacies approach, such as C. L. Hamblin,[11] J. Woods and D. Walton[12] and Johnson and Blair, to renew their efforts at developing a 'theory of fallacy'. Johnson and Blair explain:

By the theory of fallacy, we mean the attempt to formulate with clarity and rigour the conditions under which a particular fallacy occurs, along with related questions about the nature and/or existence of various kinds of fallacy.[13]

They then proceed to discuss the available literature on several of the more important fallacies. One of the most important and troublesome fallacies is that of 'irrelevant reason'.

Indeed, by any standard one of the most important informal fallacies is irrelevant reason (*non sequitur*), yet an adequate non-formal analysis of the concept of relevance has yet to be carried out. The attempts of Anderson and Belnap (and their successors) to capture the notion of relevance in a formal system have not been entirely successful. Whether non-formal analysis will fare better in this task, only time will tell. Again, the concept of adequate or sufficient evidence, as it relates to everyday arguments, requires conceptual under-pinning. And under what conditions is an undefended premise in an argument logically offensive?[14]

The lack of progress on this fallacy leaves Johnson and Blair undaunted, and they conclude the discussion by suggesting that 'a great deal of work remains to be done.'[15] However, the standstill on these related issues is extremely telling, because it strikes the Achilles heel of informal logic in general. It does not occur to Johnson and Blair that this lack of progress is not an accident, and that an account of relevance such as they require cannot, in principle, be forthcoming because canons of relevance and standards of adequacy are dependent on subject-matter. As Ennis's pragmatic dimension had emphasized, even these stan-dards must give way to contingent circumstances and possible consequences. There simply is no universal criterion of relevance, nor standards of adequacy. Thus it is not merely a matter on which 'work remains to be done'. As argued above, we have no grounds for thinking that such universal criteria could ever be identified.

Johnson and Blair cite Hamblin's book *Fallacies* as the groundwork for the development of a theory of fallacy.[16] Indeed, the book is remarkable, not only for its scholarship in tracing the history of fallacies from Aristotle (and the

Indian tradition) to modern times, but also for its perceptive account of the elusiveness of fallacies as such. Johnson and Blair suggest that research into the theory of fallacy should extend the types of initiative made by Hamblin. Hamblin's critiques of the traditional treatment of fallacies, and also of the impotence of formal logic to capture the subtleties of actual argument, are certainly persuasive.[17] But one does not find in the book grounds for sharing Johnson's and Blair's enthusiasm for a general theory of fallacy. On the contrary, aside from Hamblin's various critiques of earlier accounts, his positive theses tend to reject rather than to accept anything like a general theory of fallacy.

In particular, Hamblin proposes three distinguishable theses: first, the source and foundation of fallacies rests in epistemic considerations, not logical ones;[18] second, when it comes to the assessment of arguments, acceptance, which is relative to varying circumstances, should take precedence over such notions as validity or truth;[19] third, the rules and conventions of dialectic (that is, argument) are determined by the context and belief states of the interlocuters.[20] Each of these theses runs counter to, rather than supports, the notion of a theory of fallacy that could be taught and learned for general purposes. And even less do they support the view, advanced by Johnson and Blair, that informal logic can be used 'as a tool for the critical analysis of reasoning, and its raw material, *wherever* they occur'. Hamblin's theses, however, do support the general view advanced in this essay that the proper analysis of good reasons is functionally determined by various subjects, disciplines and forms of thought. The present essay does not, after all, reject the existence of things called fallacies or valid arguments, but only the view that their instances are universally applicable across subject areas.

Moreover, there is a sense in which Hamblin's departure from Johnson's and Blair's desideratum of a general theory of fallacy is even more radical than my own. In Hamblin's discussion of a system of formal dialectic he is prepared to countenance the view that instances of fallacies are subjective insofar as they are dependent on the belief state or commitment state of individual agents. This has the effect of rendering certain fallacies objectively character-izable but contingent in each case upon the idiosyncratic belief states of individual participants. In order properly to apply the label 'fallacy' to a given argument, one must know far more about an agent's beliefs and use of language than any theory of fallacy could possibly supply. Overt statements are not adequate indices of fallacy, and the possible contexts are infinitely variable. Thus, even Hamblin's coherent account of certain fallacies provides little ground for optimism about applying a theory of fallacy in practical situations. If anything, that prospect would now seem more remote.

One final point about Johnson's and Blair's enthusiasm for fallacies should be made here. This has to do with the importance that they seem to accord to the discovery (perhaps one should say, the creation) of new fallacies. In summarizing what they regard as progress in the field of fallacies, they say:

> Finally, completely new fallacies have been added as writers have canvassed real arguments about current issues that use contemporary ammunition and pondered the responsibilities of arguer and audience as reflective citizens or consumers. We think here of Kahane's ... 'tokenism', 'unknown fact', 'suppressed evidence' and statistical fallacies; or of Weddle's ... 'stereotyping' and 'half-truth'[21].

In fact, the list of fallacies is restricted only by our ability to find names for them, since, as argued earlier, the number of ways in which it is possible to make mistakes is virtually infinite. It is difficult, therefore, to share Johnson's and Blair's enthusiasm for the introduction of new fallacies. More generally, I have never seen any proponent of the fallacies approach address himself head-on to this objection, even though it is probably as old as Sextus Empiricus.[22] In more modern times, other writers have expressed the same view:[23]

> There is no such thing as a classification of the ways in which men may arrive at an error: it is much to be doubted whether

there ever *can be*. (A. De Morgan)[24]

Truth may have its norms, but error is infinite in its aberrations, and they cannot be digested in any classification. (H. W. B. Joseph)[25]

It would be impossible to enumerate all the abuses of logical principles occurring in the diverse matters in which men are interested. (M. Cohen and E. Nagel)[26]

Proponents of the informal fallacies approach merely bypass this point by stating that 'certain outstanding abuses' and 'popular errors' are commonly made, which they wish to clarify. However, to qualify unambiguously as one of the classified fallacies, the error must be common enough (and clear enough) for us all to recognize it as an error. But this raises serious questions about the level and type of discourse to which the fallacies can usefully be applied. Either a particular fallacy is readily identifiable, or it is arguably not one of the classified fallacies at all. A very similar objection to the fallacies approach has been made by Michael Scriven:

> One might suppose that the preceding argument [Scriven's] establishes a strong case for the 'fallacies approach'. It might, except that the fallacies generally turn out not to be fallacies – unless one builds into the identification process, and hence into the labels, all the skills needed for analysis without the taxonomy of fallacies. In that case one has made it a formal approach, and the encoding (*i.e.*, diagnosing) step has become the tricky one.[27]

In order to support their negative judgement about the usefulness of formal logic, Johnson and Blair quote Yehoshus Bar-Hillel:

> I challenge anybody here to show me a serious piece of argumentation in natural language that has been successfully evaluated as to its validity with the help of formal logic.... The customary applications are often careless, rough and unprincipled, or rely on reformulations of the original linguistic entities under discussion into different ones ... through processes which are again mostly unprincipled and ill understood.[28]

This challenge, it seems to me, applies *pari passu* to the informal fallacies approach as well. Indeed, the situation is slightly worse for, as Johnson and Blair admit, 'Of no informal fallacy can it be claimed that we now possess a widely accepted theoretical account ....'[29]

The theory of argumentation

In addition to the fallacies, the other area of research relating to informal logic distinguished by Johnson and Blair is the theory of argumentation. They state:

> By the theory of argument – the second focus of research in the journals – we mean the attempt to formulate a clear notion of the nature of argument which is not the slave of formal logical or proof theoretic models, and to develop principles of reasoning which come closer to shedding light on mundane argumentation than do those of formal logic.[30]

Again, Johnson and Blair do a creditable job of reviewing the recent literature in this area, pointing out open questions and unresolved problems as they go. Moreover, they are quite candid about the degree of success attained in these endeavours:

> In summary of research in this area, it seems that the theory of argument is not much further along than the theory of fallacy. The notions of effective argument, plausible argument, successful argument, inadmissible argument are all of them inchoate, but may be seen as initiatives in the direction of exploring a notion of argument which is closer to the domain of natural argumentation, and which may outrun the notions of validity and soundness.[31]

As a consequence of Johnson's and Blair's view (which is correct) that there is not, at the moment, anything resembling an adequate theory of argument, one is forced to consider not any existing theory but what Johnson and Blair think a theory of argument might be like and what it might be capable of doing.

From all that Johnson and Blair have to say on these questions, it is clear that for them a theory of argument would possess at least the following two properties: first, it would address itself to 'practical', 'everyday', 'real-life', 'ordinary' and/or 'mundane' argument, as distinct from formal or mathematical arguments; second, it would possess some kind of 'theoretical underpinning' that would serve to codify, systematize or organize solutions to problems in the above areas. They say, for example:

> What is needed now, in fact, is a survey of the various practical solutions that have been developed for these problems, and an attempt to fashion the necessary theoretical underpinnings.[32]

Implicitly, then, it can be seen that they view 'ordinary, everyday argument' as a clearly discernible domain over which some sort of theory of argument might reign. They cite Stephen Toulmin's book *The Uses of Argument*[33] as the most cogent, if not the first, attempt at laying the groundwork for just such a theory. Toulmin shows very clearly the inadequacies of formal logic in its efforts to do justice to actual, real-life argumentation. In addition, he shows how different fields of argument employ different types of inference 'warrants' that legitimize the move from data to conclusion. Different types of 'warrant', he argues, receive their legitimacy (or justification) in much the same way that jurisprudential laws are founded upon precedent. The study of logic, therefore, if it wishes to be practical, must take these different types of inference (or 'warrant') into account.

Johnson and Blair are correct, I believe, in citing Toulmin as perhaps the most important leader in the field of practical logic (if we can call it that). However, I think it can be shown without much difficulty that Toulmin's work does not support a theory of argument of the sort that Johnson and Blair have in mind. On the contrary, the implication of Toulmin's pioneering work is that there are as many different types of legitimate argument as there are fields or subjects that may be argued about. Inference 'warrants', for Toulmin, are always field-dependent. And fields, with their corresponding modes of reasoning, differ more widely than species of animals. According to Toulmin, formal logic made the mistake of overlooking these significant differences in reasoning. The same argument, therefore, that undermines the general effectiveness of formal logic applies with equal force to a general theory of practical logic. Toulmin's work supports the idea of multiple theories to cover the multiplicity of subjects, all with different patterns of inference. His thesis provides no encouragement for those who strive for a general theory of argument with a common 'theoretical underpinning'. Indeed, the fundamental insight behind Toulmin's thesis (quoted in chapter 2, p. 33) is that there is no recognizable entity that we might conveniently call 'everyday' or 'real-life' argument. Real-life argument is as varied and diverse as the range of human experience and interests. And when carried on intelligently, its complexity is infinitely greater than any single theory could reasonably hope to account for. The denial, or failure to recognize, this brute fact about the complexity of human discourse led the medieval formal logicians to take their calculi too seriously; now, apparently, it is leading informal logicians to make the same mistake. Thus it is not because Toulmin is wrong that I reject Johnson's and Blair's call for a theory of argument. It is because he is right.

When one stops to analyse the many 'remaining problems which require further research', painstakingly pointed out by Johnson and Blair throughout their paper, it can be seen that they all stem from the ubiquitous (though unrealistic) desire for a theory of argument with a common 'theoretical underpinning'. Some of the remaining problems are:

> How can an argument be extracted from its surrounding rhetoric?
> What principles of interpretation apply?
> What standards of evaluation are then to be used?
> How are the criteria of evaluation to be determined?[34]

Each of these problems suggests that some sort of uniform answer is expected, as though the principles will be the same in every field, no matter what the subject matter. But this is what Toulmin has argued one should not expect; and that is precisely why they persist as unresolved problems. Uniform answers to these questions, which transcend or supervene subject areas, are not forthcoming.

On the other hand, if Johnson and Blair should want to claim (despite evidence to the contrary) that they are not necessarily looking for any single theory of argument but are in fact prepared to countenance many simultaneously, then, it seems to me, the flood gates are open, and so many different types of reasoning will be found that there will be no recognizable field called informal logic. Much less will they find something that may be 'canonized as an autonomous discipline'. The existing disciplines are already steeped in their own reasoning procedures, fallible as they might be at times. But learning to use those procedures properly involves learning the idiosyncracies of those disciplines. The dilemma for informal logic is this: learning to reason *in vacuo* (that is, in isolation from specific subject areas) is as fruitless and sterile as formal logic, yet learning to reason substantively involves learning about the actual subject areas. The former choice commits the sins of the past; the latter requires the breadth of learning of a Renaissance man. The informal logician's desire to have it both ways – that is, to know how to reason within an area without knowing the area – stems from a long-held philosophical prejudice, which is that philosophy somehow has a monopoly on such things as argument, reasoning and proper analysis. But this attitude is patently ill-founded. Not only does the sophisticated reasoning of physicists, lawyers and mathematicians often outstrip philosophy's general capacity to take account of it, but also new logical systems are often constructed on the heels of these advancing disciplines to help us to understand the complex relationships discovered therein. It is arguable that philosophy could learn more about reasoning and argument from these disciplines than these disciplines could learn from philosophy. In any case, there is no justification for the claim of any single discipline to be multi-competent in all argument.

Michael Scriven and reasoning

Johnson and Blair identify Michael Scriven's book *Reasoning* as one of the 'new wave' textbooks that champion the cause of informal logic. There is little question that it is the freshest and most imaginative book to have appeared in this area for a long time. In particular, it recognizes the inherent deficiencies of the so-called 'fallacies approach' and the inadequacies of formal logic. Indeed, Scriven dismisses both approaches as inadequate for much the same reasons. His argument against both, in brief, is that by the time a student accurately and fairly 'encodes' an argument into its actual form, all the difficult work of analysis has already been done. Thus Scriven might be a champion of informal logic, but he is no friend of the 'fallacies approach'.

The major strengths of Scriven's book are the ways in which he casts off the traditional modes of argument analysis, such as the inductive–deductive dichotomy, the rules of inference and all the accompanying jargon usually associated with these traditions, and most important, its sensitivity to the imprecision and fluidity of actual human discourse. He wants his reader to see how this renders argument analysis an extremely complex business. In each chapter he reiterates such points as:

> It is not hard to see from this section the extent to which *judgement* is a crucial part of argument analysis, indeed of understanding utterances in the English language. They are often rich in meaning or in the appearance of meaning, in connotations or associations or implications, and sometimes in resounding emptiness. Indeed, it isn't possible to condemn or praise much communication without taking account of the context; what may be subtle and sensitive in one context may be superficial and uninformative in another. Judgement enters here, and judgement isn't something that can be achieved by following a simple formula.[35]

Indeed, Scriven's approach to argument analysis is so sensitive to linguistic nuance and contingent contexts that many logic teachers think he has thrown out too much of the valuable machinery of formal logic, and that one is left with too little logic. If Robert Ennis erred in trying to subject essentially human problems to the dictates of logic, then Scriven's critics might charge him with having humanized essentially logical problems. In any event, it is clear that Scriven is not prepared to make argument analysis appear more simplistic than it is; and what may have been sacrificed in terms of formal rigour is balanced by a more realistic appraisal of what is actually involved in such analysis.

Scriven does, however, offer some counsel to those with a bent for systematic analysis. He breaks down the process of argument analysis into seven steps:

1. Clarification of *Meaning* (of the argument and of its components)
2. Identification of *Conclusions* (stated and unstated)
3. Portrayal of *Structure*
4. Formulation of (unstated) *Assumptions* (the 'missing premises')
5. Criticism of
   a) The *Premises* (given and 'missing')
   b) The *Inferences*
6. Introduction of *Other Relevant Arguments*
7. *Overall Evaluation* of this argument in the light of 1 through 6.[36]

Most of the book is devoted to the elaboration of the complexities involved in applying each of these steps, together with suggestions for how this might be accomplished. For step 3, the portrayal of structure, for example, he offers a method of using tree diagrams, which help the student to organize and display the perceived relationships between premises, missing assumptions and conclusions; this method does not rely upon the traditional apparatus of formal logic, nor the so-called fallacies.

An important dimension of Scriven's book consists in his placing of the pedagogic emphasis on the delicate process of translating an actual thesis or argument, as it originally appears, into a schema that captures its basic structure. Scriven calls this process 'encoding' the argument so that its structure is revealed. He stresses the fact that this is the most difficult and most important phase of argument analysis, not only for beginners but for accomplished logicians as well. There is not much point in acquiring a facility with the rules of inference unless one can shape an argument into the form in which those rules clearly apply. Nor is there much point in criticizing an argument if it is not the actual argument that one has been offered – a 'straw man' only facilitates 'straw critiques'. As one might expect, therefore, considerable space is allocated to 'assumption hunting' or 'finding missing premises', a major problem in 'encoding'. For this problem in particular Scriven presents four criteria that 'missing premises' should satisfy; again, these criteria make an enlightened contribution to discussion in this area.

Scriven points out that the seeds of his book germinated in a course of his suggestively called 'Speed Reasoning'. In addition to this, the title of his book, *Reasoning*, suggests that Scriven considers reasoning to be a general skill. Indeed, in a chapter-end quiz we find Scriven posing the following problem to his readers:

> 1.   'Reasoning is a particular skill in using thought and language, and it is proficiency in this skill, not the mere possession of language, which distinguishes the human species from the others on this planet.'
>   a.   True (according to this text)
>   b.   False (according to this text)
>   c.   Other (explain)[37]

Scriven says that the first answer is the correct one. All of this, together with the book's general thesis, points to the view that reasoning as such is a general skill. Moreover, it is considered to be a skill that can be learned through discovering, and then practising, the various procedures and strategies that Scriven delineates. His entire book, in fact, is an attempt to teach this alleged skill.

If, however, one rejects Scriven's major assumption and believes that reasoning is not a general skill but at most a general term, then his proposals for teaching and learning it are otiose, as unhelpful as lessons in constructiveness or effectiveness, which are likewise general terms that do not describe particular skills. My reasons for rejecting the notion of reasoning (like that of critical thinking or creativity) as a general skill are these: first, the term 'reasoning' does not denote any particular process, performance or type of achievement but rather a variety of them; second, the variety of things that we can and do reason about is so diverse that no one set of skills can produce competence in reasoning about all of them; third, we can, at best, teach people how to reason in specific areas and in connection with specific types of problem, but the various types of reasoning have too little in common to be considered a single skill. I would, therefore, be suspicious of any book that purported to teach reasoning *simpliciter*, just as I would be suspicious of one that claimed, without qualification, to teach intelligence or thinking. Thus I do not accept the premise on which Scriven's book is based.

However, early on in his book we find Scriven backing away from his initial claim to teach reasoning as such and switching to the more restricted and quite familiar endeavour of teaching argument analysis. From the consumer's point of view, this type of 'baiting and switching' no longer causes much alarm. We have grown used to it as a consequence of the oft-repeated suggestion of logicians that the two are in fact the same thing. However, reasoning and argument analysis are not identical; in many instances the two have little in common. Indeed, it is arguable that the type of reasoning that educators want to promote and individuals to practise, has little or nothing to do with argument analysis – particularly as that is envisaged by informal logicians. More often than not, educators want to teach, and people to learn, methods for solving the problems that confront us. It is of comparatively little interest that particular pieces of reasoning can be reconstructed *ex post facto*, for purposes of analysis, by those who are peculiarly inclined to this pursuit. This is not to suggest that argument analysis is not, at times, important to our deliberative efforts; it is merely to point out that it constitutes a comparatively small proportion of it. I do not, therefore, think the switch from talking about reasoning to talking about argument analysis should be accepted lightly, because it tends to bury a very fundamental distinction and bestows upon argument analysis a power that it does not possess. (One practical consequence of this confusion has been the proliferation of textbooks on the subject.)

Even if, following Scriven, we restrict ourselves to argument analysis as such, it can be seen that this approach to reasoning and critical thinking still fails to achieve its objectives. Indeed, this is as true of other informal logic approaches as it is of Scriven's. The reasons for this general failure, I believe, have a common source (ironically, the same source as that which led informal logicians initially to reject formal logic as a guide to practical reason). This is the view, which has always been the mainstay of formal logic, that the form of an argument is more important than its content. This assumption continues to be shared, whether consciously or not, by the informal logic approach as well. If this were not the case, the whole notion of argument analysis as a special subject for abstract study would be entirely without content. Indeed, for formal logicians, who are interested in studying the deductive relationships between abstract formulae, this assumption is particularly apt. But for informal logicians, who are concerned with the evaluation of practical reason for daily affairs, the assumption is not only counter-intuitive but also needs considerably more justification than has ever been found for it. In fact, I believe this assumption to be the major stumbling-block to effective argument analysis. In brief, it fails to recognize that (as biologists would put it) the form of good arguments follows their function.[38] The opposite assumption is made by informal logicians. They, like their counterparts in formal logic, attempt to devise uniform standards but must pay the price of general effectiveness. They continue to insist that, regardless of subject matter, context or specific purpose, all good arguments should conform to some finite set of teachable rules or principles. The diversity of arguments and their purposes shows this idea to be untenable.

As already indicated, Scriven's approach to argument analysis is more sensible than most, insofar as it tackles the practical problems of analysis that students actually confront. Needless to say, I am not as sanguine as he that the difficulties of argument analysis can be overcome merely by practising the exercises that he sets, in particular, those that cover his seven steps of argument analysis. I think it instructive, therefore, to consider some of the difficulties that inhibit the success of these steps specifically and of this approach in general.

First, it is important to notice a general feature about the seven steps themselves, which is inconspicuous but in fact undermines their practical efficacy. The seven steps are laid out and presented by Scriven (see above, p. 83) as though they were seven discrete and sequential steps that must be practised, or at least treated, independently. In fact, however, these alleged steps are neither discrete nor sequential; the accomplishment of each is contingent on the satisfactory resolution of them all. Appearances aside, they are not steps but rather a single, cohesive entity.

Consider, for example, the first four steps, which occupy the lion's share of the procedure. They are, again:

1. Clarification of *Meaning* (of the argument and of its components)
2. Identification of *Conclusions* (stated and unstated)
3. Portrayal of *Structure*
4. Formulation of (unstated) *Assumptions* (the 'missing premises').

In real-life arguments it is not possible to accomplish accurately any one of the above steps without having simultaneously met the requirements of the others. You could not, for example, be sure of the meaning of an argument and its components unless you could identify the conclusions (stated and unstated), since otherwise you could not be sure of where the argument was trying to go and hence ensure that you had its 'meaning' right. Nor, conversely, could you identify the conclusions unless you understood the meaning of the argument and its components. Very often in argument, as in the analysis of normal English paragraphs, the real meaning or point of the discussion is left unstated and must be inferred by the reader or listener. The most accurate guide we have for making inferences about the meaning and conclusions of an argument is to check the one against the other. This gives us the clearest picture of each; for without this guide we are merely groping in the dark about possible meanings and possible intended conclusions.[39]

The mutual dependence of these two steps can be seen in Scriven's own instructions to the reader on these points. For example, in order to 'clarify the meaning', he suggests:

> (e.) Write out any important unstated but intended implications or suggestions of the premises, the conclusions, and the argument or passage as a whole. (What's it trying to get across that isn't actually spelled out?)[40]

Yet, for the following (second) step, 'identifying conclusions', we are advised:

> (b.) To locate the stated conclusions, look for indicator words like 'therefore', 'because', 'so', and 'thus', and for placement cues such as location at the end of a paragraph. (These cues are by no means always reliable: you also *have to depend on your sense of the meaning of the passage as a whole*).[41]

He continues:

> (c.) Notice that there may be several conclusions in the argument, each building on the previous ones. And a passage may also contain several entirely separate arguments.[42]

These instructions, for allegedly different steps, clearly rely upon one another: indeed, they effectively duplicate one another. In no meaningful sense can they be considered independent, discrete steps.

The reciprocal dependence of step 3, 'Portrayal of Structure', and steps 1 and 2 is perhaps even easier to perceive. The instructions for step 3 involve, as before, separating premises from conclusions. Again, therefore, this is not a significantly different nor discrete step. Other aspects of mutual reliance among these alleged steps would be easy to demonstrate. The point is that argument analysis might be described by identifying different steps, but it cannot in truth be carried out in independent steps. These alleged steps are integrally linked in a network of mutually dependent assumptions, meanings and implications, which must be viewed together in order to be understood. Much less are these steps sequential. We are offered the illusion that argument analysis consists in following a step-by-step procedure, but in fact it is a continuum of all these dimensions (and more) simultaneously. We could no more analyse a real-life argument by using Scriven's steps sequentially than we could form an idea of the taste of a pudding by sampling its ingredients individually in the order dictated by the recipe.

At first glance my rejection of Scriven's steps of analysis may appear to mark no more than a relatively minor pedagogic difference between him and myself. It may seem, for example, that since Scriven is describing real components of argument analysis, it is of comparatively little importance that they are not discrete steps. However, my criticism is not quite so trivial: if Scriven's steps are not discrete nor sequential, then the objection has very serious implications for his book in particular and the teachability of argument analysis in general. The absence of steps goes to the heart of argument analysis as a plausible subject for study. It suggests that courses that promise mastery in such analysis are either over-zealous or simple-minded.

Scriven on 'assumption hunting'

Scriven's step 4, 'Formulation of (unstated) *Assumptions* (the "missing premises")' has long been the source of difficulties for informal logicians in general. Scriven, therefore, devotes considerable space to addressing these issues, and his contribution in this area has been praised by Johnson and Blair, among others. The problem has been to determine what particular assumptions a given argument is making, since no argument is complete as it stands. These assumptions, moreover, must be supplied without doing violence to the initial argument or creating a 'straw man'. Theorists of informal logic, therefore, have been trying to develop objective and teachable criteria for supplying missing premises. Without such criteria, there is no way of knowing whether one is analysing the actual (or initial) argument with which one is confronted.

Much of Scriven's discussion about missing premises is not new, and leaves the problem essentially unresolved. However, his original contribution to the problem consists in providing a criterion for distinguishing between 'significant' and 'insignificant' assumptions and in arguing that only the former should be added.

> The crucial point about an extra premise, one that we're going to *add* to the ones that are already visible, is that it should bring to bear *new, relevant,* and *convincing* evidence.... The requirement that the extra or 'missing' premise (which is what an assumption is) be *new* immediately precludes a mere repetition of the supposed connection between the given premises and the required conclusion. There's nothing new about the statement that what is already being provided is supposed to give support to what is alleged to be the conclusion of the argument. So, typically, an assumption should be referring to something else that hasn't been directly mentioned in the given premises, and connecting it with some important concept that occurs in the conclusion.[43]

The question is: does this requirement of bringing in new evidence really help to resolve the problem of finding missing premises? It would appear, in fact, to raise as many difficulties as it purports to resolve.

To begin with, there is a clear difference between analysing a particular, given argument and requiring that one introduce 'new, relevant, and convincing evidence' to it. Does the argument not then become a significantly different one, even though the conclusion remains the same? There are, after all, numerous arguments that can support a given conclusion: some of these arguments may be strong and some weak. The same is true of missing assumptions. Our job, however, is to analyse the argument with which we were presented, or at least a very close approximation to it. To ignore this basic responsibility is to license, if not to encourage, all manner of fanciful interpretations. It is difficult, therefore, to see how one could conform to Scriven's requirement that one introduce 'new, relevant, and convincing evidence' without doing violence to the actual argument given. The only instance in which to follow Scriven's advice would not be to damage an argument would be that rare case in which just one assumption is possible. But most things in the world of events or ideas are not like that. Just as there is more than one way to get through a forest and more than one set of events may bring about a given effect, so there are usually several possible assumptions that might support a given conclusion.

This is not to suggest that in assessing an argument one does not have to consider other pertinent evidence that might bear on the conclusion; indeed, to ignore such evidence would be irrational. But the process of introducing fresh evidence to an argument has crucial consequences for any planned programme or method of argument analysis. The first of these is that we cannot claim that the new evidence is a *de facto* assumption of the argument because we usually have no independent way of knowing this: all we can claim about such evidence is that it effects our assessment of the argument as a whole (either positively or negatively) *whether or not it is being assumed*. In short, we can accept or reject arguments for reasons that we find compelling, but we cannot know if these reasons are in fact being assumed by the argument.[44] There is a subtle but important distinction between assessing a conclusion and analysing an argument. We should be candid about the fact that we can (and do) assess conclusions even when we have no objective methods for determining assumptions.

Second, Scriven admits that 'assumption hunting' (as he calls it) is not a mechanical procedure but requires 'imagination and creativity' on the part of the analyst. However, I do not think that the implications of this admission have been sufficiently realized. It acknowledges, in effect, that at the heart of argument analysis there is no method and at bottom one is left to one's own devices. While Scriven's suggestions rule out some strategies as unreasonable, ineffective or unfair, they cannot be said to have provided a positive method for argument analysis, as promised. Creativity and imagination are the antithesis of method.

More significantly, however, Scriven's admission that argument analysis and 'assumption hunting' require creativity should prompt us to recognize that dispassionate analysis cannot be guaranteed or safeguarded. When, for example, we introduce new evidence or information to an argument, we should recognize that the information is always selective. With a suitable selection of different information or alternative assumptions, the opposing case might well be defended. In general, I would argue that in the abstract it is always possible to render any argument vulnerable if the analyst cooks it right by bringing in certain choice assumptions or putatively missing premises. Nor can constraints on creating a 'straw man' prohibit this phenomenon: it is simply a straightforward result of bringing new evidence to bear on an argument. A person simply introduces the evidence that he or she sees as most fitting, and what a person regards as fitting is not dictated by any method or rules of argument analysis. The infiltration of biased or opinionated evidence cannot be prevented. Thus the major attraction or promise of argument analysis is not fulfilled. It seems to offer us an objective, dispassionate procedure for resolving arguments in a methodical way, but it cannot deliver this. Its initial enticement, therefore, is also its major disappointment.

I would like to make it clear that I do not defend, nor do these arguments support, any form of relativism that holds that arguments can prove anything they want, therefore formal procedures for resolving them are a waste of time. Rather, this is merely to point out that arguments normally take place within complicated networks of circumstance and purpose, and removing them from these contexts (for purposes of analysis) is intellectually dangerous because there is no effective method for doing so. I am not against the assessment of arguments (indeed, this is unavoidable): I am simply against the claim that there are more or less routine methods for doing it.

One final point about the introduction of new evidence should be noted here because it clearly demonstrates a major thesis of the present essay. This has to do with the important role played by extra-argument information in the analysis and assessment of arguments. If one looks, for example, at Scriven's own analyses of extended arguments, it can be seen that he follows his own advice and introduces 'new and relevant evidence' to the arguments. Indeed, this new evidence is often sprung on the reader in a surprising way, thus having the dramatic effect of apparently undermining a given argument.[45] What Scriven does not draw attention to, however, but needs to be emphasized, is the extent to which this new evidence depends upon having access to, and understanding, technical information that is not part of the argument itself. No amount of skill nor lengthy practice at argument analysis can provide information. Yet it is an essential ingredient of effective argument analysis. Scriven, like others before him, diminishes the importance of knowledge and information in order to stress his alleged skills. This emphasis, however, overlooks the fact that the best assessments of arguments usually come from people with the most information about a subject and not from those merely skilled in argument analysis. In a world of complex facts, events and ideas there simply is no short cut to analysing arguments apart from understanding these complexities. And understanding of the required sort is not easy to come by. I do not think we are helped by being led to think otherwise.

NOTES

1. Ralph H. Johnson and J. Anthony Blair, 'The recent development of informal logic', a paper presented at the Symposium on Informal Logic, University of Windsor, Ontario, 26 June 1978. The *Proceedings* were in press at the time of writing. All references to this paper are taken from the original typescript as presented at the time. The book has now been published, however, under the title *Informal Logic: The First International Symposium* (Inverness, Cal.: Edgepress, 1980).
2. Englewood Cliffs, N.J.: Prentice-Hall, 1959.
3. New York: McGraw-Hill, 1976.
4. I have always found it curious (and unjustified) that informal logic books discuss 'the fallacies' with a touch of paranoia, as though mistakes in reasoning were always perpetrated by unscrupulous souls who are out to deceive. Witness, for example, these titles: Nicholas Capaldi, *The Art of Deception* (Buffalo, N.Y.: Prometheus Books, 1975), Michael Gilbert, *How to Win an Argument* (New York: McGraw-Hill, 1980), R. H. Johnson and A. J. Blair, *Logical Self-Defense* (New York: McGraw-Hill, 1980), K. W. Fearnside and W. B.

Holther, *Fallacy: The Counterfeit of Argument* (Englewood Cliffs, N.J.: Prentice-Hall, 1959). All of these view fallacies as deceptive tricks. Whatever happened to honest mistakes made by normal people trying to do their best? At least Aristotle made it clear, in *Sophistical Refutations*, that he was discussing deliberate sophistry.

5. Originally published as *La nouvelle rhétorique: traité de l'argumentation* (Paris, 1958).
6. *op. cit.*
7. *ibid.*, p. 3.
8. *ibid.*
9. This point was argued at length in chapter 2.
10. This excludes, of course, cutting across the formal deductive sciences to areas of empirical inquiry.
11. *Fallacies* (London: Methuen, 1970).
12. 'On fallacies', *Journal of Critical Analysis*, vol. 4, no. 3 (October, 1971), pp. 103–12.
13. 'The recent development of informal logic', p. 11.
14. *ibid.*, p. 13.
15. *ibid.*
16. Published in London in 1970.
17. For an interesting critique of Hamblin's *Fallacies*, see John Woods and Douglas Walton, 'On fallacies'.
18. *Fallacies*, pp. 72–7.
19. *ibid.*, pp. 242–5.
20. *ibid.*, pp. 283–4.
21. 'The recent development of informal logic', p. 34.
22. See *Works*, vol. 2: *Against the Logicians*.
23. All three of the following statements are taken from Hamblin, *Fallacies*, p. 13.
24. In *Formal Logic* (London: Taylor and Walton, 1847), p. 276.
25. In *An Introduction to Logic* (Oxford: Clarendon Press, 1916), p. 569.
26. In *Introduction to Logic and Scientific Method* (London: Harcourt, Brace and World, 1934), p. 382.
27. *Reasoning*, p. xvi.
28. 'The recent development of informal logic', p. 14.
29. *ibid.*, p. 13.
30. *ibid.*, pp. 13–14.
31. *ibid.*, pp. 16–17.
32. *ibid.*, p. 30.
33. Published in Cambridge in 1958.
34. 'The recent development of informal logic', p. 29. There is a much longer list of such problems in their Appendix, p. 53.
35. *Reasoning*, p. 156.
36. *ibid.*, p. 39.
37. *ibid.*, p. 7.
38. This point, that different field-dependent arguments generate their own appropriate standards of evaluation, constitutes the thesis of

Stephen Toulmin's *The Uses of Argument.*

39. Scriven's warning to the student (*Reasoning*, p. 40) that 'The meaning of an argument (or word, or other expression) is not what the arguer *intended* but what he or she *said*' does not avoid this difficulty because this advice presupposes that words or expressions have one meaning only, which is independent of a speaker's intent or peculiar context. Wittgenstein (in *Philosophical Investigations*) and I. A. Richards in *The Meaning of Meaning* (New York: Harcourt, Brace, 1956) have shown that this is not the case, however.

40. *Reasoning*, p. 40.

41. *ibid.*, p. 41. The italics are mine.

42. *ibid.*, p. 41.

43. *ibid.*, p. 173.

44. Nor is the strategy of making 'minimal assumptions' particularly helpful here because it fosters the illusion that there is but one reasonable assumption. It is also possible that Scriven is here confusing the notion of a presupposition with that of an assumption, although these notions are logically different from one another.

45. The analysis that Scriven offers on pp. 169–73 of *Reasoning* is a particularly good example of this.

CHAPTER 5

Edward de Bono
and Thinking

All lessons are lessons in thinking.[1]

In 1973 Edward de Bono announced that 'between 250 and 300 primary schools, village schools, secondary modern, comprehensive, public and grammar schools, and Further Education Colleges (representing about 200,000 pupils) will be treating "thinking" as a subject in its own right.'[2] At present the large attendance at his numerous workshops and the widespread use of his classroom materials indicate that his popularity in school circles continues to increase. This is perhaps more true in Britain than in North America. Nonetheless de Bono's popularity is significant on both sides of the Atlantic. The very titles of his books (such as *Thinking Course for Juniors, The Five-Day Course in Thinking, Children Solve Problems, CoRT Thinking Lessons* and *Teaching Thinking*)[3] seem to offer the perfect solution to every teacher's problems. This promise, together with his easy-to-use 'workbooks' for teachers, no doubt account for the wide grass-roots adoption of these materials. It is surprising, therefore, that de Bono's work has not received the scrutiny that one would expect from professional philosophers of education and others concerned with the development of critical thinking.

Although de Bono's work on thinking includes numerous books and articles, there are really only two strategies that lie behind his plans for improving the teaching of thinking: the CoRT (Cognitive Research Trust) thinking materials and lateral thinking.

Throughout de Bono's work are various polemics opposing the traditional academic approach to knowledge and academics in general. Academics, he observes, typically 'struggle to find thoughts to keep up with their stream of words'.[4] But what makes de Bono even more of an academic maverick is the total absence in his work of any footnotes or references that would support any of his claims and, generally, the lack of indexes. This is especially serious when his claims are clearly of an empirical nature, and his argument rests on them.[5] This fact alone may explain why traditional academics have never taken his work very seriously.

There is nevertheless a more serious side to de Bono's thought that makes his rejection of, and separation from, academia almost complete: his rejection of what he calls 'the verbal tradition in education', which, he claims, began with Thomas Aquinas and has been epitomized more recently by Wittgenstein. He charges that the 'verbal tradition' (that is, thinking in language) has contaminated our productive thinking capacity by emphasizing debating skills over original thinking. The medieval preoccupation with the meanings of words and concepts has reduced our conception of thinking to 'semantic coherence'.

> Our academic institutions, probably because they were established by the ecclesiastic authorities, have much too great a respect for semantic thinking. There is also a more practical reason for this reverence. A person who directs his thinking at words rather than at what they describe always feels in control of the situation. There is no further data that he would like to have, his data can never be shown to be wrong or insufficient. So an academic sitting in an academic tower never need descend to examine the vagueness of the real world where complete data are impossible. Instead he examines the semantic consistency of the argument, the words themselves rather than the thoughts which the words so imperfectly convey. This leads to logic-chopping, nit-picking, nun's knitting and all the metaphysical gymnastics that result.[6]

Putting aside the fact that academics, like de Bono, intend to use words to express thoughts, and that de Bono's own words are not specially marked 'real thoughts' (as against 'semantic coherence'), there is an interesting thesis here. This is that propositional knowledge, the mainstay of academic scholarship, is a restricted, if not deficient, form of human knowledge, and that another kind of non-propositional knowing should replace it. Such a view constitutes a definite challenge, if not a threat, to our usual approaches to scholarship and learning. Unfortunately, de Bono never develops, nor argues for, this point of view. The one characteristic of his work consistent with this thesis is the fact that his texts, workshops and learning materials are extremely visual (as against verbal) in form. He repeatedly asserts that drawing and visual expression are more natural media both for expressing thoughts and for solving problems. Indeed, his own workshop demonstrations for teachers consist largely of quickly drawn pictures and diagrams, and some contain nothing but pictures with a brief comment at the bottom.[7] Presumably, these materials are to stand as cases in point to prove that traditional verbal (that is, academic) learning stifles creativity and clear thinking, while drawing and visual learning promote them.

On the surface at least, it would appear that in areas such as engineering, architecture, mechanics, design and perhaps art, de Bono may well be correct, though more argument is needed. In other, less graphic areas, however, he is arguably wrong. In any case, such a mundane observation would not support anything like a new epistemology or form of knowledge, as de Bono implies. And since he neither articulates nor defends the strongest interpretation of his apparent view, no critique will be offered of it beyond raising a query about the 'visualness' of literature, history, mathematics, ethics and politics, not to mention foreign languages. It may be that a picture is worth a thousand words, but a thousand pictures do not make one assertion. But then, de Bono might say, these are just words!

The mechanics of mind

As a justification for his curriculum proposals, de Bono advances a thesis about the brain and its various thought processes in his book *The Mechanism of Mind*.[8] The theory as presented, however, bears little resemblance to de Bono's description of it elsewhere. For example, in *Teaching Thinking* he describes the content of *The Mechanism of Mind* as providing 'a description of the *actual mechanism of the brain* as a self-organizing information system'.[9] And teachers are told that this 'description of the brain's workings' forms the foundation of his prescriptions and programmes on 'thinking'. Yet the first four chapters of *The Mechanism of Mind* are spent artfully explaining that the 'actual mechanics' of the brain are not known, and that it is not particularly important or necessary that we know the 'actual mechanism' anyway. While this latter point may be true, it nevertheless renders his justification of thinking programmes to teachers as misleading as the book's title itself. Rather than a description of the mechanics of the brain, what he presents are several conflicting models of, and metaphors for, how we may conceive of the brain working. Indeed, his book would have been more accurately entitled *Metaphors of Mind*, since, as de Bono admits, 'In this book the function of the brain system is not described with words but with working models.'[10]

> At the end of this first half [of the book] the mechanism may be compared to a large piece of paper with writing on it. The paper is in the dark and across its surface moves a small pool of light as from a flashlight....
> The second part deals directly with how the brain thinks, how people think. The second part arises from the first as a flower arises from its stem. The purpose of the stem is to bear the flower. Without a stem only an artificial flower can survive.[11]

I am afraid, however, that in lieu of being shown ' how the brain thinks, how people think', we are given several artificial stems, as well as flowers, in the form of numerous metaphors for the brain. We are asked to liken the brain's functioning to any number of things:

> A number of pins are stuck just far enough into a white board
> for them to stand firmly upright. On the heads of the pins is
> laid a thin polythene sheet which covers the whole board. This
> is the memory-surface. The input to this memory-surface
> consists of drops of coloured water which are sprayed from
> above on to the polythene sheet....[12]

This model is introduced to explain passive memory. But,
recognizing the need to explain the phenomena of the
interaction of information and ideas, de Bono constructs
yet another fictitious entity called the 'special memory-
surface':

> One needs a model in which a pattern put on to a surface will
> leave a permanent trace that will affect the next pattern that is
> put on to the surface. In this way, the contours of the surface
> will be a sculpted record of all that has happened to the
> surface.[13]

In order to provide this, de Bono further suggests:

> An ordinary table jelly made up in a shallow dish provides just
> such a model. The flat surface of the jelly is virgin memory-
> surface. The incoming pattern is hot water spooned on to the
> surface at different places.[14]

Elsewhere, we are asked to conceive of the brain as one of
those advertising displays that print moving words with
thousands of bulbs (his 'thousand bulb model') to explain
the 'flow' of ideas and memories. And further metaphors
are introduced to explain other brain functions and modes
of thought.

Aside from the disappointment that results from
learning that the 'description of the actual mechanism of
the brain'[15] reduces to a series of metaphors, there are two
criticisms of de Bono's models or metaphors that are more
serious. The first has to do with an implicit inference that
de Bono makes regarding the truth or plausibility of his
models. He claims:

> The validity of ideas [that is, the models] is not proved by the
> way they come about, but once they have come about then

they might prove to be valid in themselves ....

Even though no formal attempt is made to prove that the information-processing system described is the one operating in the brain, there is evidence to suggest that it may be. The actual details of the system may be different, but the broad class of system is probably the same.[16]

The implicit argument can be restated as follows:

> *Premise:*   If these models of the brain functioning are correct, then we could explain thinking, remembering and forgetting in certain ways.
>
> *Premise:*   We can explain thinking, remembering and forgetting in these ways.
>
> *Conclusion:* Therefore these models are (probably?) correct.

However, this line of reasoning is formally invalid. Technically, it is an example of the fallacy of affirming the consequent (that is, $P \supset Q$, $Q \therefore P$). It is possible to construct n number of models of the brain that might account for our thinking as we do, but our thinking as we do does not provide grounds for believing any particular model to be the correct one. And given that de Bono presents no physiological or other corroborating evidence of any kind, we are left with a mere model and no grounds for believing it.

The second major criticism of de Bono's thesis is the alleged connection between his model of the brain and his prescriptions for improving our thinking through such devices as CoRT, lateral thinking and PO.[17] If, as de Bono claims, the brain is made up of 'mechanical units' and *The Mechanism of Mind* was written to provide 'a description of the actual mechanism of the brain', then we are left to wonder how our deliberate, volitional choice can seriously affect this mechanism. For, as de Bono says, 'In this book the brain is described as the mechanical behaviour of mechanical unit.'[18] De Bono admits that underneath his functional models is a physiological reality that determines its peculiar functioning. This raises a serious question: how can lateral thinking, PO and all the rest cause the brain to work in a manner that is mechanically different from that prescribed by de Bono's models? What Cartesian pineal gland enables our volitional deliberation to change the basic 'mechanical behaviour of mechanical units'? De Bono's prescriptions for the CoRT materials, lateral thinking and PO effectively attempt to have the brain work in a way that is physiologically different from the way in which the model says it must work. This is not to deny the inherent merit or usefulness of de Bono's educational prescriptions but merely to point out that his model of the mind is at cross purposes with his prescriptions and cannot serve as a foundation for them.

Thinking

In that thinking, as such, is the *raison d'être* of de Bono's many books and educational proposals, one would expect to find a fairly clear idea of what thinking is to emerge from his work. Instead one finds many different definitions and descriptions of thinking spread throughout his work:

> What happens in the brain is information. And the way it happens is thinking.[19]

> Thinking is the flow of attention along the d-line pathways.[20]

> Thinking is a device to enlarge our perception.[21]

> In this book thinking will be regarded as a sort of internal vision which we direct at experience in order to explore, understand and enlarge it.[22]

> Thinking is the deliberate exploration of experience for a purpose.[23]

> Thinking is the operating skill through which intelligence acts upon experience.[24]

> I would define thinking as 'moving from idea to idea to achieve a purpose'.[25]

While suggestive, the definitions suffer from a lack of precision. For one thing, if thinking is a skill, as de Bono claims that it is, it is not at all clear how these vague descriptions, taken singularly or collectively, could be adequately distinguished from the rest of our mental processes. Perhaps the tacit recognition of this prompted de Bono to caution us:

> It is best not to have any preconceptions and to let the intangible subject of thinking gel into something definite and usable in the course of the book.[26]

But the caution does not merely effectively undermine his own definitions; it also makes it practically impossible to determine whether de Bono ever makes good his claim that

> This book is about a particular approach to the subject of thinking itself, and a practical approach to the teaching of thinking.[27]

How can one determine whether one has taught thinking successfully when it is not clear what the skill is? There are two sources of de Bono's vagueness (and apparent duplicity) on this matter of teaching thinking. First, he assumes that thinking is a generalized skill; second, he actually promotes a particular or specific type of thinking that differs considerably from what most people, and certainly educators, usually mean by thinking.

That thinking is assumed to be a generalized skill is revealed in statements such as the following:

> The aim is to produce a 'detached' thinking skill so that the thinker can use his skill in the most effective way.[28]

And that this general skill is also considered capable of being directly taught is manifest in the way de Bono's materials are advertised:

> Can children be taught to think, not as a by-product of learning some other subject, but directly and deliberately in special 'thinking' classes? If they can, does it really benefit them, in school and in the world outside? The answer this book gives both those questions is a clear Yes.[29]

De Bono, however, does not appear to recognize the logical connection between his view that thinking is a generalized and teachable skill and his failure to provide an adequate definition of thinking. His reluctance to settle upon a single definition of thinking stems from the tacit acknowledgement that there are many different types of thinking. It is a pity that he does not see that the wide variety of thinking skills, which defy accurate and singular definition, is also what implies that thinking is not a generalized skill. There are simply too many types of thinking, manifest in diverse skills, to permit us to infer a single generalized ability for their respective achievement. Just as a good builder of sandcastles is not necessarily a good builder of everything from mathematical models to Utopian societies, so a good thinker in one area does not possess a generalized skill applicable to all areas.

My earlier arguments (see chapter 1) were designed to show that critical thinking is not a generalized skill either, and that it makes no sense to claim that one teaches critical thinking as a generalized skill. If the restricted term 'critical thinking' cannot reasonably refer to a generalized skill, then the wider term 'thinking' can hardly do so.

The second source of de Bono's vagueness about teaching thinking stems from his confusion of the particular type of thinking (that he has in mind) with thinking in general. In *Teaching Thinking*, for example, he promises a general method for teaching thinking *simpliciter*:

> The book is intended to deal in a practical and personal manner with the teaching of thinking. It is not philosophical speculation, but is based on what may well be the largest programme anywhere in the world for the direct teaching of thinking as a skill and, quite apart from this, on considerable experience in the teaching of thinking to somewhat demanding pupils. Above all I should like the book to be of use to teachers who want to teach thinking directly as a skill.[30]

However, what one finds in *Teaching Thinking* (and, for that matter, in his other books) are not methods for teaching thinking but rather suggestions for how to generate different or unique hypotheses – what psychologists call 'divergent thinking' or 'generative thinking'. It is the type of thinking that is often associated with creativity, and de Bono often uses the terms interchangeably. But although this particular type of thinking is often useful and sometimes important, it is a long way from capturing the diverse and polymorphous phenomenon that we call thinking. More important, it is even further away from the type of thinking that teachers usually (and properly) see themselves as being concerned with. The reading teacher is properly not concerned with the student's ability to concoct an alternative alphabet, nor the history teacher with his ability to invent a different name for the Battle of Waterloo. The point here is not to discuss the relative merit of teaching 'divergent thinking' or 'creativity', but to note that de Bono promotes it as something that it is not, namely, the generalized 'teaching of thinking directly as a skill',[31] as though one might acquire universal thinking competence by following his instructions. This is not to say that de Bono's lessons and practice drills do not require thinking (bingo and dishwashing require thinking too); it is to suggest that his materials do not come close to delivering the skill that is advertised on the package.

CoRT thinking lessons

In recommending his specific proposals for teaching thinking, de Bono first criticizes some of the traditional methods used for getting students to think. Before turning to the CoRT materials directly, it is important to consider his criticism of logic (and its teaching) in particular, because it is the primary justification for the CoRT materials.

> It must be admitted that logic is a good way of teaching logic. It must also be admitted that most of the developments in the teaching of logic have been internal developments arising from the subject itself, and not from considerations of its practical applicability as a thinking tool. As has been discussed at various points in this book, logic is only part of thinking. The direct use of the deductive process forms only a very small part of ordinary thinking. The emphasis upon it in education arises from the type of artificial problem that is so

often used. In such problems all the information is given and some basic principles can be applied. In real life, information is very rarely complete and there may be no basic principles at all. The main deficiency of logic is the starting point. Where does one start? ...

The rules of logic do matter, but unfortunately the perfection of the subject does not guarantee its usefulness as a practical way of teaching thinking.[32]

And elsewhere he correctly points out how unfortunate it is that:

When one sets out to teach thinking as a skill one finds that the 'logic' concept has been so long established that it is at once assumed that one is trying to teach logic. ... In some cases ... the term logic has been expanded to include anything that is to do with thinking and is correct and useful. This is a dangerous situation because the meaning of the term 'logic' has come to embrace all of thinking, but the actual process remains confined to the rules of formal logic. This extreme type of 'capture' occurs with many other long established concepts.[33]

Several similar criticisms of logic appear throughout de Bono's work, and they can be summarized as follows:

1　logic is often wrongly thought to be synonymous with effective thinking;
2　formal logic requires that all the relevant information be given at the start, but most real problems are not like that;
3　logic cannot introduce new ideas, pose alternatives, nor cope with novel situations.

Basically, I think de Bono correct on all three points. However, his solution to these deficiencies – that is, the CoRT thinking materials – does have serious short-comings.

The name of de Bono's thinking programme, CoRT Thinking, 'derives from the initials of the Cognitive Research Trust'.[34] The complete CoRT course is designed for children between nine and sixteen years old and consists of a series of subject-neutral 'operations', or exercises, through which the students are supposed to develop 'tools' for transfer to any problem requiring thinking. The new focus here is that these operations are designed to improve thinking in what de Bono calls the 'perceptual' phase of thinking, in contrast to the 'processing' phase, in which logic and other conventional strategies can be employed. How a person perceives a problem is every bit as important as how he resolves it once it is clearly seen. These different phases of problem solving have been labelled by others[35] as the 'context of discovery' and the 'context of justification' respectively. De Bono, then, is properly focusing his attention on precisely that area of problem solving where logic is notably deficient – the context of discovery.

> Most of practical thinking takes place in the perception state and not the processing stage. People react to things as they see them and the way they see them determines the nature of the reaction. So the basic method could be called the 'spectacles method' – that is to say, if you help pupils to see situations more clearly then their reactions will be more appropriate.[36]

De Bono's exercises, or 'operations' constitute the so-called 'spectacles' through which a student is taught to see a problem before venturing an answer or a solution. The 'operations' are intended to provide students with strategies for generating plausible ideas and hypotheses before they 'process' a solution.

The operations are so simple and straightforward that only a few of them need to be illustrated. The first CoRT 'operation' is called PMI (for Plus, Minus and Interest). The students are first given an artificial problem by the teacher; for example, 'Consider the proposition "All automobiles should be painted yellow".' The students are directed, either in small groups or individually, to spend five minutes considering the 'plus' factors for the proposal, five minutes considering the 'minus' factors and then a few minutes considering 'interesting' points about the proposal. For the teacher the point of this lesson is to get the students to understand and practise PMI as a thinking procedure. Their answers are not the important part of the exercise; the essential point is the PMI thinking 'operation'. The objective is to have this PMI thinking procedure become sufficiently crystallized in the child's mind that it can be transferred to other problem-solving or thinking situations.

Another CoRT thinking 'operation' is CAF (Consider All Factors). Again, students are given a problem or proposition and asked to generate as many factors as possible that might be relevant to the problem. With practice, they begin to construct progressively longer lists of factors than they could before training. The emphasis is upon extending the breadth of the students' consideration and not upon arriving at right or wrong answers. De Bono considers that the CAF lessons develop a generalized skill that is transferable to virtually any problem.

FIP (First Important Priorities) is another of the dozen or more 'operations' in the CoRT thinking course:

> The FIP operation is of importance in such situations as making decisions or in planning. In both these situations it may be a matter of balancing one thing against another and to do this one must decide the importance or priority of each of the things. For instance in choosing a job one may have to balance the pay that a certain job will offer against the enjoyment of that job. ... The emphasis of the lesson is on deciding which things are important....[37]

The directives to teachers in this instance is to get students to internalize the following set of questions as a set drill or 'thinking operation':

> What are the important things here?
> What are the priorities? (As before the word Priority should be introduced as much as possible rather than avoiding it.)
> Which of these things are the most important? ...
> Which things matter most?[38]

Again, FIP is an 'operation' that, according to de Bono, the student can apply to virtually any thinking situation that must issue in a decision or plan.

All of the CoRT thinking 'operations' are thus designed to emphasize the process, rather than the content, of thinking. The successful student should be able to use these crystallized skills on nearly all practical problems, according to de Bono. De Bono also refers to these 'operations' as 'attention-directors', meaning that once a student has mastered them, they serve to focus attention upon the many ways in which a problem can fruitfully be thought about or 'perceived'. While de Bono makes any number of claims about the virtues of the CoRT thinking 'operations', essentially they reduce to three.

1   They constitute a set of 'generalized thinking skills' that are independent of content and transferable to virtually all problem areas regardless of content.
2   These skills can be likened to a set of 'neutral spectacles' that enable students to 'perceive' problems more clearly (for example, in the context of discovery).
3   Nearly everyone can learn these operations since they presuppose no prior knowledge or information.

As de Bono says, 'In the CoRT thinking lessons pupils can operate at once since the only resources used are already available within their heads.'[39] This last feature of this programme requires our attention because it contains the key to some of the major problems with CoRT.

In his admonitions to potential teachers of CoRT, de Bono is at pains to point out how subject-matter content, such as that associated with the familiar teaching of maths, science, history and literature, gets in the way and actually hinders the development of thinking. If we want students to be aware of the *process* of thinking. de Bono argues, then it must be taught in · isolation from content and information.

'If a person is thinking about something then surely he is learning how to think.'
    Unfortunately this is not true. A geography teacher would claim that in learning geography a pupil would be forced to think. A history teacher and a science teacher would make the same claim. All would be right. The question is whether thinking about something develops any transferable skill in

thinking. In 'content' subjects, the momentum of the subject is usually such that little attention can be paid to the actual process. Exhortations to 'think about it' or to consider 'what these things imply' merely ask the pupil to delve more deeply into his knowledge and find the right answer. In a content subject you cannot really think ahead of the content, because your speculation must always be inferior to the actual facts. There is comparatively little scope for thinking except of the hindsight variety: 'Now you can see that this happened because of that and that ....' This is no fault of the teacher. It is the nature of content subjects that is at fault.[40]

It is not clear what de Bono means here by the ability to 'think ahead of the content', nor whether it would be desirable to do so if one could, but it is plain that he regards traditional 'content subjects' as inferior instruments for developing the capacity to think. His major argument for this is that thinking via subjects is not conducive to the transfer of skill, whereas CoRT, putatively, finds its *raison d'être* here:

> Using thinking in particular situations develops thinking skill in those situations, but not a transferable skill in thinking. Skill has to be person-centred, not situation-centred. The dilemma is that it is usually possible to teach only situation-centred skills. You train a person to behave in a certain way in a certain situation. The way out of the dilemma is to create situations that are *themselves* transferable. We call such situations *tools*. A person is trained in the tool situation. He learns how to cope with the tool. The tool and his skill in using it can now be transferred to new situations.[41]

The idea behind teaching CoRT then is to get away from content by creating artificial situations and problems so that the 'operations' become transferable tools. This is why de Bono always uses hypothetical or fictitious examples like 'All automobiles should be painted yellow', and hundreds of similar problems that have few, if any, prerequisites for 'content'.

It is ironic that de Bono's prescriptions for removing subject content and creating artificial problems should approximate precisely the features of formal logic that he himself has so aptly criticized. What was logic's vice turns out to be CoRT's virtue. The trouble with formal logic is:

> the deductive process forms only a very small part of ordinary
> thinking. The emphasis upon it in education arises from the
> type of artificial problem that is so often used. In such
> problems all the information is given and some basic
> principles can be applied.[42]

The only difference is that CoRT provides virtually no
information and no criteria for telling when its principles
(that is, its 'operations') are being appropriately applied. De
Bono is quite adamant that teachers should encourage all
responses and should never say, 'That is wrong'. At least
logic has clear criteria for this.

With respect to skill transfer, which presumably is
CoRT's greatest strength, there is no evidence whatever
that the skills attained in the use of CoRT 'operations'
transfer to other types of problems that differ from those
in the CoRT lessons. In de Bono's favourable reports of
tests that he ran to compare CoRT-trained students with
'untrained groups', three telling points should be noted:
first, as all of the problems set were of the CoRT type, his
results are anything but surprising; second, none of the
questions is such that a wrong answer is even possible;
third, the quality of response is never quantified – only the
quantity of responses is recorded. These last two points
about de Bono's scoring procedures are important because
they reveal something fundamental about the CoRT
programme as a whole.

In all of the CoRT exercises and 'operations' *truth* is never
at issue: all that appears to matter is numbers of responses
and lists of more or less plausible suggestions. In general,
the CoRT programme subtly discredits the task of seeking
truth in academic study and in daily living as well. In most
situations in life, and certainly in academic studies, the
validity of one's thinking is far more important than the
number of suggestions one can produce. In CoRT the
examples do not require knowledge and information, and
being right or wrong is irrelevant. In his advocacy of so-
called 'thinking skills' de Bono berates the schools for
putting so much emphasis upon 'mere knowledge and

information'. He seems to minimize the difficulties of conveying 'mere knowledge and information' to adults, let alone children. A 'mere' fact or piece of information such as 'The minister resigned because of political pressure from his constituency' or 'Gravitational forces cause tidal changes', may take a competent teacher weeks to convey. And it is no mean achievement. Moreover, the type of thinking required for such understanding is what teachers and schools properly see as their responsibility.

There is a fundamental disagreement between de Bono and the advocates of traditional school subjects. Where de Bono thinks that 'content subjects' hinder important thinking, others (including myself) would argue that the disciplines are actually its constituents. Whichever way one decides the question, it is important to recognize that nothing short of an entire philosophy of the curriculum is at issue. Witness, for example:

> If children can already think so well at this age, then surely the long years of education must develop this ability to a high level. Not so. At the end of education there has been no improvement in the thinking ability of children – in fact there has actually been a deterioration. This opinion is based on experiments involving several thousand people all of whom had benefited from higher education. It is an opinion which seems to be shared by others who have considered the matter. Why should education have this effect on thinking ability?[43]

On the other hand, most people believe, and not without foundation, that the traditional disciplinary modes of thinking are the most worthwhile in the long run. For all of their shortcomings, the disciplinary traditions do represent very powerful ways of thinking about, learning about and viewing the world. They are not merely stagnant collections of 'information' or 'content' as de Bono implies. They too are *ways of thinking*. However, de Bono believes that because disciplinary thinking is tied to content, it is inherently inferior to CoRT thinking, which is not so tied. We are led to believe, moreover, that content actually inhibits important thinking, and that there is a deterioration of children's thought as a result.

There is nothing wrong with suggesting radical revisions of existing school curricula, even when those revisions entail the rejection of long-standing intellectual traditions. But de Bono's proposals are not directly presented this way to teachers; nor is it clear that he sees such implications himself. Whether or not he is aware of this conflict, I believe it has its origin in two sources: first, his attempt to inject school subjects with novelty and originality; second, his belief in the existence of 'generalized thinking skills' – skills that are not dependent upon content. However, the price to be paid for novelty and/or originality is a proportionate de-emphasis on knowledge or truth seeking, as we have come to understand this through the disciplines. There is no inherent value in novelty or originality if they do not result in some productive end. In the extreme, novelty for its own sake is chaos. With respect to 'generalized thinking skills' of the kind that de Bono envisages, it has already been argued in earlier chapters of this book that there is something incoherent about the very idea of such skills. There are instead various types of thinking skills, which are logically connected to various activities, subjects and tasks, but these are not generalized.

Also, when anyone promises to change our perceptions by providing us with a new set of 'spectacles', a familiar claim in intellectual history, we should be aware that the intended changes are not mere additions to the *status quo*. If (and I stress *if*) the changes are in fact what they promise, then something presently valued must be given up. With regard to CoRT, de Bono explains:

> the basic method could be called the 'spectacles method' – that is to say, if you help pupils to see situations more clearly then their reactions will be more appropriate. Spectacles are neutral and in the CoRT lessons there is no attempt to impose or change values (though these may change as the result of better vision). In practice for 'spectacles' we may read 'methods for directing attention'.[44]

Effective 'spectacles', however, are not epistemically neutral. If 'spectacles' produce changes in the way things are 'perceived', then knowledge has a different empirical foundation. The issue here is not the changing of children's moral and political values, as de Bono intimates, but rather the changing of teachers' educational values, the kind of thinking that teachers should regard as most worthwhile for a child's education. The issue is anything but neutral. Teachers already have 'methods of directing attention' and a tradition of knowledge worth directing attention towards. These are the values that de Bono's 'neutral spectacles' would effectively change.

Let us consider whether the change in perception is worth the gambit. In the CoRT 'operation' called CAF children are given a problem, and, either alone or in groups, are asked to list all the factors that bear upon the problem. But what sort of factor should appear on the list? What is a factor? De Bono states:

> There should not be any philosophical attempt to decide exactly what a factor is and when something is a factor and when it is not. A factor is quite simply something that should be thought about in connection with the situation. If you like you could call it a consideration or something that has to be considered.[45]

Not only does this not answer the question, but it is not a philosophical definition of 'factor' that is being sought – though that would be interesting! Quite simply, what is being sought by both the teacher and student is guidance as to what may be considered relevant to a given problem. And whereas CoRT simply backs off to let the student decide that, the traditional disciplines provide a broad range of relevant considerations.

Indeed, this is precisely why subjects like science, history and the like are so valuable; they teach people what kinds of thing are and are not relevant to a given problem – what a factor is. Contrary to de Bono's contention that 'content subjects' are not the place to begin on a problem, I would argue that they at least limit the range of plausible hypotheses. Traditional 'content subjects' likewise provide 'spectacles', but spectacles that have been ground by thousands of years of human experience. And competent teachers try to provide students with those 'spectacles' so that they might *perceive* what factors are relevant.

In the CoRT 'operation' called FIP the student is supposed to identify those elements of a problem that should take precedence by addressing himself to the questions that we have already noted:

> What are the important things here?
> What are the priorities? (As before the word Priority should be introduced as much as possible rather than avoiding it).
> Which of these things are the most important?...
> Which things matter most?[46]

To each of these questions, however, a student or teacher might legitimately reply: Important for what? Are aesthetic priorities to take precedence over functional ones and moral priorities over legal ones? De Bono answers such questions with his characteristic simplicity: 'In most situations the matters to be considered are already evident, and it is a question of assigning importance and priority.'[47] But this simply will not do. What is deemed a priority in a given situation is highly contingent upon an agent's purpose. What is a priority for one person or task might not be so far as the next. If it were literally true that 'In most situations the matters to be considered are already evident', then the whole point of the exercise is unclear. I suspect that de Bono's pedagogical warning that 'the word Priority should be introduced as much as possible rather than avoiding it' unwittingly contains the only point to the exercise: to teach the meaning of the word 'priority'. But this hardly qualifies as a generalized thinking skill.

The CoRT 'operation' called PMI suffers from the combined difficulties of CAF and FIP. Like CAF, PMI depends upon background knowledge and information to give the student some idea about what might be a plausible 'plus' or 'minus'. If knowledge is not required, as de Bono suggests, then there is no way to distinguish between good and poor suggestions. More important, there is no way of distinguishing a 'plus' from a 'minus'! And as in the case of FIP, what is to count as a priority, or 'plus' in this case, is highly contingent upon one's peculiar purposes. For example, given that 'All automobiles should be painted yellow', in order to make plausible suggestions (in contrast to all the logically possible ones), a person would have to know something about not only the intended purpose of the suggestion but also the availability and cost of such a quantity of yellow paint – not to mention aesthetic and environmental considerations! He would need not precise information about any of these but knowledge in order to understand that such things are relevant considerations. Without such knowledge, there is no way to distinguish the class of plausible suggestions from the class of logically possible ones; there is no way to distinguish a real 'plus' from a real 'minus'.

If, on the other hand, de Bono intends merely that students should list their subjective likes and dislikes as 'pluses' and 'minuses', then PMI is of limited use in contexts where truth matters (that is, in most academic studies and practical affairs), and it runs the risk of giving the false impression to students that productive thinking consists largely in being clear about one's subjective preferences. Similar difficulties reside in the other CoRT operations such as C and S (Consequence and Sequelae), and AGO (Aims, Goals, Objectives), but I shall not criticize them here. I wish only to give the reader some sense of the kind of 'spectacles' that de Bono offers teachers. For myself, I find the 'spectacles' particularly opaque and much harder to see through than traditional methods for getting students to think.

There remains one final, general criticism of CoRT. Despite all of de Bono's advance warnings that CoRT is meant to improve 'perceptions in the perceptual stage and not the processing stage', he has in fact confused and combined these two stages (the 'context of discovery' and the 'context of justification': the 'context of discovery' refers to the generation of ideas or new ways of looking at things, and the 'context of justification' refers to the judgement or proof of those ideas once generated).[48] However, many CoRT operations, in particular CAF and PMI, clearly require judgement about the acceptability of ideas or proposals. Indeed, in de Bono's own discussion about the virtues of PMI it can be seen that people's judgement is supposed to be affected by the 'operation':

> If a random half of a group of people are asked to give their opinion on a situation then they will give a definite judgement. If the other half are asked to do a deliberate PMI and then give a judgement it is found that the judgement after the PMI is really rather different from the judgement before PMI. This means that a deliberate attempt to look at the good and bad points has actually changed the judgement of the group.[49]

However, changing the judgement of the group has little to do with suggesting an idea in the 'perceptual stage' and a great deal to do with the acceptability of an idea in the 'processing stage'. A similar criticism can be made of CAF. The reason why it is desirable to 'consider all factors' about X is to make an idea more acceptable as a judgement about X, but this is clearly 'processing' an idea in the context of justification.

Perhaps the clearest indication of de Bono's confusion of the 'processing' and 'perceptual' stages of thinking can be found in his own misgivings about the use of the word 'perception' for the CoRT operations.

> As will be come apparent in this book, we also need a much better word than 'perception' for the-way-we-look-at-things. Perception is too abstract, too psychological and too concerned with visual and other sensory perception to cope with the way the *mind* looks at things. One day I may find the right word for this, but I do not have one yet.[50]

De Bono, of course, is correct. Perception is 'too psychological and too concerned with the visual'. But if he were aware of the vast literature available on the 'context of discovery' *versus* the 'context of justification', he would see that his distinction need not be so contaminated.[51] As it is, the word 'perception' points to the very real muddle that pervades the CoRT programme. The programme does collapse the distinction he wants to make between the two contexts, and that is why the word 'perception' correctly strikes him as odd and unfortunate. Initial perception and judgement are different things. Moreover, this is precisely why the CoRT operations, when abstracted from subject content, are empty and superficial in the context of discovery and would be absolutely useless as methods of justification.

Lateral thinking

Lateral thinking constitutes the final unit of the CoRT programme, but de Bono has also written four separate books about lateral thinking[52] and considers it a distinct topic. Lateral thinking describes those methods of thinking that introduce new ideas, or the type of thinking that we normally associate with inventiveness and creativity. It differs from the other CoRT 'operations' in that it does not purport to be a better way of thinking about normal problems but is rather specifically intended for generating new ideas and unorthodox solutions. Unfortunately, it is impossible to find a clear statement of what lateral thinking is that is free of de Bono's sales talk for it. He comes closest to defining what it is when insisting on what it clearly is not:

> Lateral thinking is quite distinct from vertical thinking which is the traditional type of thinking. In vertical thinking one moves forward by sequential steps each of which must be justified. The distinction between the two sorts of thinking is sharp. For instance in lateral thinking one may have to be wrong at some stage in order to achieve a correct solution: in vertical thinking (logic or mathematics) this would be impossible. In lateral thinking one may deliberately seek out irrelevant information: in vertical thinking one selects out only what is relevant.[53]

Elsewhere he summarizes the difference as follows:

> vertical thinking [is] high-probability, straight-ahead think-ing, and lateral thinking [is] low-probability, sideways thinking.[54]

If and when a low-probability idea works or leads to something, the pay-off is far richer in terms of its usefulness than ideas whose implications are obvious. Often lateral thinking attempts to generate new ideas just for their own sake and not necessarily for the solution of any known problem. Thus lateral thinking might be described as an attempt to codify certain procedures and techniques that generate new ideas.

De Bono claims that lateral thinking is not intended to challenge or replace our conventional methods of 'vertical' thinking but rather to supplement them. But perhaps because lateral thinking is intended as a corrective for both the known limitations of formal logic and the tendency of people to pursue non-productive lines of conventional thought, it is, unfortunately, perceived by the general public, and particularly by educators, as a replacement for conventional thinking. Moreover, despite his statements to the contrary, de Bono's own prefaces, dust-jacket blurbs and occasional discussions do much to foster this misinterpretation of his work. He does not clarify sufficiently what the real intent of lateral thinking is and what it is not.

The essence of lateral thinking is to avoid looking at familiar patterns and to connect features of ideas or objects that are not normally associated. As de Bono says, 'We want to move *across* tracks sometimes, not along them';[55] hence, the term 'lateral thinking'. He describes lateral thinking as composed of an attitude and a method for using information in unusual patterns. The attitude is 'Let's look at an idea to see where it gets us' because, he suggests, 'the value of an idea is where it leads, not what it describes at the moment.' The method consists in a series of different strategies and techniques for thinking about problems. These strategies range from familiar 'brain-storming' techniques to de Bono's techniques of 'concept challenge' and 'random stimulation'. 'Concept challenge', for example, involves taking some commonly held assumption or a familiar object such as a walking stick and trying to restructure its parts, function or design into some new and potentially useful pattern. 'Random stimulation' consists of taking virtually any arbitrarily selected object or word and working back from it through associations to some initial problem or situation. The selected word is called a 'stepping-stone idea'. The rationale here is that when one is bereft of solutions to a problem, the introduction of a strange word will carry associations and analogies of its own, and in principle any two ideas can be connected in some way. Very often, de Bono claims, these connections are productive of potential solutions or at least of ideas that might be of interest for their own sake.

'PO' is a quasi-word that de Bono introduces to render lateral thinking more accessible in practical situations. The word 'PO' can be interjected into sentences in place of a noun, an adjective or a connective and is intended to convey the same meaning as the words 'possible' or 'perhaps'. Sample uses might be 'PO planes land upside-down', or 'Penalties for PO crimes on Monday are double'. That PO itself is not a word, nor the resulting sentences always grammatical, is a virtue, according to de Bono, because where language leads to familiar thoughts and pattens, PO jars them and compels fresh and unusual associations. The most important characteristic of PO is that it always stands in contrast to NO, which, according to de Bono, is the operative word of logic and conventional thinking.

> Although both NO and PO function as language tools the operations they carry out are totally different. NO is a judgement device. PO is an anti-judgement device. NO works within the framework of reason. PO works outside that framework. PO may be used to produce arrangements of information that are unreasonable but they are not really unreasonable because lateral thinking functions in a different way from vertical thinking [sic]. Lateral thinking is not irrational but arational. Lateral thinking deals with the patterning of information not with the judgement of these patterns. Lateral thinking is prereason. PO is never a judgement device. PO is a constructive device. PO is a patterning device. The patterning process may also involve depatterning and repatterning.[55]

Note the curious mix of explication and rhetorical persuasion that de Bono uses to promote his ideas. In this instance, to be critical of PO is like being critical of 'constructiveness'– if that is possible.

In this instance at least, de Bono does not confuse lateral

thinking with the 'context of justification'. It is clearly a thinking tool for the 'context of discovery'. However, one must be wary of generalized prescriptions for thought within the 'context of discovery' that are totally independent of subject areas. Of necessity such prescriptions must disregard peculiarities of content and knowledge, which in fact provide ideas with their plausibility. Without some kind of content-dependent guidelines, lateral thinking could produce an infinitely large collection of literal nonsense. De Bono advises the lateral thinker to disregard normal clues and patterns so that the 'traps' of conventional 'vertical' thinking can be avoided. For this reason a more accurate name for lateral thinking would be 'lateral guessing'. De Bono should have no objection to such a change except that the term would lose much of its rhetorical punch. Educators, however, would be less apt to construe lateral thinking as something that it is not. They could see better how far it departs from what one would normally regard as thinking.

Even 'lateral guessing' remains guessing. What is worse, it is uninformed guessing. De Bono frequently attempts to establish the usefulness of lateral thinking by suggesting that many famous scientists and inventors – men such as Einstein, Edison and Pasteur – have used it. Basically, his argument is that these men, particularly Edison and Pasteur, discovered too many things to attribute their good fortune to chance. Instead, de Bono argues, they had the 'habit of mind' to make the most of chance happenings or accidental ways of looking at things, which is none other than lateral thinking in rudimentary form.

> Inventors and famous scientists usually produce a string of new ideas, not just one. This suggests that there is a capacity for generating new ideas that is better developed in some people than in others. This capacity does not seem to be related to sheer intelligence but more to a particular habit of mind, a particular way of thinking....
>
> With practice in looking at things in different ways the capacity to find a context for any given bit of information increases to a remarkable extent. As one gets better at lateral thinking, chance offerings of information, chance con-

junctions of ideas, come to be more and more useful. It is not
that chance itself has changed, but simply that one gets better
at harvesting it.[56]

The glaring deficiency of this explanation, however, is that
it totally fails to consider the extent to which these men
were steeped in the knowledge and information of their
respective fields. They did not perceive their 'chance
offerings' in an informational vacuum. As Pasteur himself
once said, 'Chance favours the prepared mind.' What de
Bono has failed to see is that this preparation does not
consist in a peculiar 'habit of mind' called lateral thinking,
but in being thoroughly immersed in the knowledge and
data of one's field. When one is in command of such
information and data, then one is prepared to recognize
'chance offerings' for what they are and to capitalize on
them. Many people had isolated oxygen before the
prepared mind of Lavoisier recognized it for what it was.
And many people had seen moulds grow on citrus fruit
before the prepared mind of Fleming recognized its
potential as an antibiotic. De Bono is correct in saying that
such people can harvest the 'chance offering' better than
most people but wrong in suggesting it is because of a
special ability with lateral thinking. Theirs is a capacity for
'vertical' thinking that follows after thorough preparation
with the knowledge of their field. Such preparation is a
prerequisite for discoveries of this magnitude, and lateral
thinking offers no short-cut to significant discoveries.

Finally, there remains a serious epistemological problem
with the use of lateral thinking. Just as one would not
conduct expensive experiments to find out something
about which information is easily available in the nearest
library, so one would not use lateral thinking until one had
first exhausted 'vertical' thought. 'Vertical' thought is by
definition (as de Bono would admit) more direct and
reliable. But learning how to use conventional 'vertical'
thought is a complex and time-consuming task, and
learning when to use it in many instances requires asking a
lot of questions or doing a lot of research. To be rational, all
of this should be done first. One does not reach for the

explosives until one has tried the latch on the door. Such considerations militate against the initial use of lateral thinking. In a practical context it will always be difficult to decide when it is rational to use lateral thinking. Problems do not come marked 'soluble' or 'insoluble'. One finds out this information through normal, 'vertical' means. This shows, as argued earlier, that normal, 'vertical thinking' is epistemically prior to lateral thinking. The schools, for all their faults, are correct in focusing upon this priority. Unfortunately, many teachers apparently feel (and I stress *feel*) that de Bono's various thinking programmes are providing their students with bright, shiny, new thinking skills. They should be reminded that all that glitters....

NOTES

1. Gilbert Ryle, 'A puzzling element in the notion of thinking', in P. F. Strawson (ed.), *Studies in the Philosophy of Thought and Action* (New York: Oxford University Press, 1968), p. 23.
2. 'But how do you teach thinking?', *Times Educational Supplement*, 17 August 1973, p. 4.
3. *Thinking Course for Juniors* (Blandford Forum, Dorset: Direct Educational Services, 1974); *The Five-Day Course in Thinking* (New York: Basic Books, 1967); *Children Solve Problems* (Harmondsworth: Penguin, 1972); *CoRT Thinking Lessons* (Blandford Forum, Dorset: Direct Educational Services, 1974); *Teaching Thinking* (London: Maurice Temple Smith, 1976).
4. *Thinking Courses for Juniors*, p. 6.
5. For example, he justifies the child's use of drawings (in place of words) merely by asserting that 'Visual expression is much less an acquired skill than verbal expression', *ibid*.
6. *Teaching Thinking*, p. 38.
7. See, for example, *Children Solve Problems* and *The Dog Exercising Machine* (New York: S & S, 1971).
8. Harmondsworth: Penguin, 1971.
9. *Teaching Thinking*, p. 37 (emphasis added).
10. *The Mechanism of Mind*, p. 36.
11. *ibid.*, pp. 9–11.
12. *ibid.*, p. 61.
13. *ibid.*, p. 97.
14. *ibid.* p. 97.
15. *Teaching Thinking*, p. 37.
16. *The Mechanism of Mind*, p. 39.
17. PO is a term coined by de Bono in one of his programmes to

stimulate thought about alternative possibilities; thus PO describes a type of thinking. See his *PO: Beyond Yes and No* (Harmondsworth: Penguin, 1972).

18. *Mechanism of Mind*, p. 7.
19. *ibid.*, p. 18.
20. *ibid.*, p. 155.
21. *Teaching Thinking*, p. 20.
22. *ibid.*, p. 32.
23. *ibid.* pp. 95–6.
24. *ibid.*, pp. 32–3.
25. *Thinking Course for Juniors*, p. 6.
26. *Teaching Thinking*, p. 17.
27. *ibid.*, p. 17.
28. *ibid.*, p. 50.
29. From the widely reproduced dust-jacket of *Teaching Thinking*.
30. *Teaching Thinking*, pp. 7–8.
31. *ibid.*, p. 8.
32. *ibid.*, pp. 103–4.
33. *ibid.*, pp. 95–6.
34. *ibid.*, p. 111.
35. See chapter 1, p. 14–15.
36. 'But how do you teach thinking?', *Times Educational Supplement*, 17 August 1973, p. 4.
37. *Ibid.*
38. *Thinking Courses for Juniors*, pp. 96–7.
39. 'But how do you teach thinking?', p. 4.
40. *Teaching Thinking*, p. 104.
41. *ibid.*, p. 108.
42. *Teaching Thinking*, pp. 103–4.
43. *Children Solve Problems*, p. 9. Again, notice the absence of any references for the study he alludes to here.
44. 'But how do you teach thinking?', p. 4.
45. *Thinking Courses for Juniors*, p. 91.
46. *ibid.*, p. 97.
47. *ibid.*
48. I should like to make it clear that I am discussing those CoRT 'operations' that are *exclusive* of lateral thinking.
49. *ibid.*, p. 94.
50. *Teaching Thinking*, p. 9.
51. This again, is a result of de Bono's admitted refusal either to read or to footnote work done in his own field.
52. The four books are: *The Use of Lateral Thinking* (Harmondsworth: Penguin, 1971); *Lateral Thinking: A Textbook of Creativity* Harmondsworth: Penguin, 1977); *Lateral Thinking for Management* (New York: McGraw-Hill, 1974); and *PO: Beyond Yes and No*.
53. *Lateral Thinking*, p. 11.
54. *The Use of Lateral Thinking*, p. 139.

55. *Lateral Thinking*, p. 197.
56. *The Use of Lateral Thinking*, pp. 20, 104.

CHAPTER 6

Reading, Testing and Critical Thinking

This chapter will examine the two most commonly used tests for measuring critical thinking: the Watson–Glazer Critical Thinking Appraisal and the Cornell Critical Thinking Tests. It will be argued that neither test in fact measures critical thinking in any reasonable sense because, first, neither the tasks nor the results of these tests show any significant difference from those involved in 'general intelligence' (that is, IQ) testing and, second, the restrictive format of the tests precludes the use of critical thinking in any defensible sense of that term. Aside from the fact that these tests fail, however, our understanding of the concept of critical thinking can be illuminated by examining the precise reasons for these failures. In particular, the difficulties involved in testing for critical thinking have very much in common with some of the more traditional problems associated with testing for basic reading, literacy and reading comprehension. The parallels that exist between these two areas of testing are so striking at times that their comparison helps to elucidate these difficulties and hence the nature of critical thinking.

Reading research

The available literature on the teaching and learning of reading is perhaps the most voluminous of all areas of educational research. However, if one restricts oneself to

126

that area of reading research which addresses the question 'What *is* reading?', two general observations are immediately possible. First, there is far less agreement on this basic question than one would expect; second, a researcher's view of what reading is greatly influences the type of research that he or she does in the area. Indeed, in many instances it is possible to tell what a researcher's view of reading is simply by examining the type of question that the research is supposed to answer.[1]

With a few exceptions, it is possible to categorize or classify reading researchers into one of two different types, according to the implicit view of reading embedded in the research strategy. Both groups begin from the point at which a basic language facility has already been acquired, as in the case for most school-beginners. The first group, which is by far the largest, appears to regard reading ability as the possession of certain symbolic 'decoding and pronunciation' skills, sometimes simply referred to as the 'letter-sound code'. This group typically deemphasizes the more advanced problems associated with reading comprehension and focuses on such things as phonics, perception (for example, of whole words or parts), vocalization, sub-vocalization, auditory discrimination, memory span and other technical skills thought to be necessary for reading. It is, incidentally, among this group of researchers that the phonics *versus* whole word controversy rages. In general, however, this entire group seems to regard reading as a set of basic ('decoding') skills; for this reason we can refer to its principles as the 'basic skills approach'.

The other group of researchers is less sanguine about the prospects of the basic skills approach, principally because it regards reading as far more complex than any set of isolatable skills.[2] For this group the cognitive prerequisites for reading comprehension are fundamental to the reading process, and, since comprehension involves *understanding* information, concepts and various implications of these, the 'basic skills' view is overly simplistic. From this point of view, reading cannot be divorced from comprehension because they are not separate but one and the same act. The research of this latter group continues to raise fundamental questions about the nature of reading and treats it as a complex cognitive achievement. We might refer to this perspective on reading as the 'comprehension approach'.

As an acid test for differentiating between these two approaches to reading, we might pose the following question: is it possible to read X without comprehending (that is, understanding) X? The latter group of researchers would clearly say, no, it is not possible; indeed the major thrust of their research efforts is designed to point this out. For them the nine-year-old who fluently 'decodes' sentences from an advanced political treatise cannot, for this reason, be said to be reading. The 'basic skills' group, however, is at best ambiguous about this question. Its emphasis on perception, vocalization, memory span and the like suggests that reading consists in properly 'decoding' the 'letter-sound code'. It is not clear whether 'decoding' for them entails comprehension. And if it does, to what extent is comprehension involved? They might say, for the sake of argument, that 'decoding' involves comprehension, but their substantive research relegates it to a minor role. It would appear that every effort is made to keep reading within the domain of basic, more or less mechanical skills. For if this is not the case, the floodgates of comprehension would render reading far more complex than is neatly manageable.

M. Wiener and W. Cromer[3] have introduced a distinction between the skills that might be necessary for the acquisition of the skill of reading itself and those necessary for accomplished reading. They point out that those concerned with acquisition are likely to stress 'identification' skills (for example, 'decoding'), while those interested in accomplished reading are likely to stress comprehension. This is a useful distinction, since it helps to explain the different research emphasis and also how the two conceptions of reading become entrenched. Moreover, it is worth heeding their subsequent warning that the two research endeavours should not be confused. But useful as this distinction is, it does not vitiate the conceptual link between reading and comprehension. Whether a person is an accomplished reader or just a beginner, his ability to derive meaning from print, which is what reading is, is limited by his ability to *interpret the message with understanding.* This, indeed, is what comprehension means. The point cannot be avoided that whatever else reading involves, comprehension is part of it. It might be possible to 'decode' without comprehension (a nine-year-old could, for example, merely articulate the sentences from *Paradise Lost* correctly), but it is not possible to read without comprehension.

Some researchers, following the 'basic skills approach', attempt to bypass the complexities associated with comprehension by arguing that learning to read is a different task from learning the language, and comprehension is a function of understanding the language.[4] There are, after all, articulate adults who cannot read. But this observation merely forestalls the inevitable realization that language, and the knowledge thereof, is likewise an integral function of being able to read. Many English-speakers with knowledge of no other language, for example, can 'decode' printed German sentences with excellent pronunciation. Are we prepared to say that these people are *reading* German? I think not. The whole purpose of reading is to receive a message from the printed symbols. If proper letter symbols provide no message, there is no comprehension, and if there is no comprehension there is no reading in any intelligible sense of the term.

Thomas G. Sticht has shown how the truncated conception of reading (that is, the 'basic skills approach') seems to have won the day in the most widely used tests for basic literacy.[5] His objection to these tests is that literacy, like reading comprehension, should be regarded as more than the mere ability to 'decode' printed words or sentences:

> Evidence abounds that indicates that there is currently considerable lack of consensus as to what literacy means, and how knowledge, reading, and literacy interrelate. For

example, here is an item from the National Assessment of Educational Progress: Reading (1972).

The person being tested is presented the following sign:

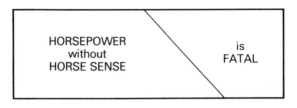

They are then asked: Where would you probably see this sign? (They are given the instructions to mark the correct alternative.)

		Per cent Correct by Age			
		9	13	17	Adult
On a highway	X	23.3	44.6	75.7	88.4
On a gymnasium floor	___				
At a racetrack for		64.3	47.2	17.6	7.0
horses	___	(Per cent choosing this alternative)			
In a grocery store	___				
I don't know	___				

The point to remember about this item is that it occurred within an assessment battery that purports to assess our nation's achievement in *reading*: those who marked the third alternative would be scored incorrect and their reading capability, and hence the nation's reading capability, would be challenged. Yet in this study, and others like it of recent vintage ... there is no check to find out whether lack of reading skill or lack of specific knowledge is the prime reason for lack of correct performance on many items.[6]

As one might expect from this, Sticht goes on to argue that knowledge of facts, customs, social norms and the like is intimately related to what we mean by literacy. Thus literacy and reading comprehension share a common feature, namely, that they cannot be reduced to a few more or less mechanical 'decoding' skills, and that achievement in these areas requires some independent knowledge of the subject domain. Sticht's research on literacy, then, supports the 'comprehension approach' to reading, since it effectively draws the same conclusions regarding the connection between general knowledge and reading ability.

Regardless of one's view about basic reading skills, however, I think it can be seen that reading comprehension, when considered in its full-blown sense, implies the presence of some complex ingredients that go beyond mere letter-sound articulation. In particular, it implies the appropriate processing of information and the making of *inferences* with respect to that information. Indeed, with this observation in mind, the parallel with critical thinking can easily be seen. Critical thinking, after all, likewise entails the appropriate processing of information and the making of inferences with respect to that information. But as with reading comprehension, critical thinking cannot be reduced to a few mechanical 'decoding' skills.

Researchers in critical thinking, such as Ennis, D'Angelo and Scriven, have adopted a 'basic skills approach' to critical thinking in the same way as their counterparts in reading research. They have construed the problem of critical thinking as being one of 'basic skills' and have similarly de-emphasized or eliminated the complexities of interpreting and processing information (comprehension). The received opinion about critical thinking is thus that it is a collection of basic skills, as though it were merely a kind of 'letter-sound decoding' problem. Logic courses, both formal and informal, have been thought to contain the code that is constitutive of critical thinking. In the fields of both reading and critical thinking the 'basic skills approach' can only be defended by adopting a severely truncated conception of their respective processes. However, the truncated conception of reading in particular leads directly to the problems associated with literacy, such as those identified by Thomas Sticht. We should now look at how a severely restricted conception of critical thinking similarly undermines the validity of the Watson-Glazer and Cornell Critical Thinking Tests.

The Watson–Glazer test*

The Watson-Glazer Critical Thinking Appraisal (Forms YM and ZM) is the most widely used standardized test for measuring critical thinking ability available in the published literature. In addition to its most common uses as a pre- and post-test for courses in critical thinking, there are 109 published reports and studies that have used it as an official yardstick for measuring critical thinking.[7] However, close examination of the test itself and of the normalized data used to support it reveals that it has serious deficiencies, which vitiate its integrity as a test of critical thinking. First, within the test itself there are numerous muddles and confusions that actually preclude the use of critical thinking in any defensible sense of the term. Second, the extensive database amassed by Watson and Glazer does little or nothing to show that critical thinking, as a unique or peculiar set of skills, is in fact being tested.

The confusion that exists within the test first appears in the accompanying manual for prospective testers and then is perpetuated throughout the test, in various forms, by providing directions that should not in fact be followed. Indeed, in some instances the directions cannot logically be consistently followed. The confusion I refer to here stems from Watson's and Glazer's vague understanding of what an inference is. In particular, they have confused the long-established distinction between a proposition, which may be true or false, and an inference, which may be valid or invalid. They do not seem to understand that inferences are not the sorts of thing that can be true or false.

---

* *The contents of the Watson-Glazer test are the property of Harcourt Brace Jovanovich, New York. Not all the items discussed above will necessarily appear in present or revised versions of the test.*

Inferences are either valid or invalid and should never be described as 'true'. Witness, for example, their description of an inference, as described in the manual for the test:

> *Inference.* (Twenty items) Samples ability to discriminate among degrees of truth or falsity of inferences drawn from given data.[8]

In addition to the confusion noted above, this statement also introduces the equally odd (if not incoherent) notion of truth and falsity as having degrees. Normally, we speak of our knowledge or certainty as possessing degrees, but not truth or falsity. Thus one confusion is here compounded with another.

Before showing the specific way in which this basic confusion manifests itself in the Watson–Glazer test itself, it is necessary to make an observation about the logic of test questions in general. In particular, I want to draw attention to the fact that some test problems require the test taker to bring to bear knowledge or information that is outside, or additional to, the information provided in the test question itself. By contrast, there are other types of test question that are self-contained and do not require the test taker to employ outside information. Examples of these latter questions might be found in IQ tests, basic reading tests, logic tests, some types of maths tests and the like. An example of the first of these two types of problem, that requiring outside or additional information, might be:

Test statement:
Wage and price controls constitute 'tampering' with the free-market forces by Government. This often results in some inequities and also slows the economy.

Corresponding question:
Should Government desist from infringing on free-market forces and stop all forms of wage and price controls?
Answer: ? (Maybe.)

An example of a self-contained test problem, requiring no outside or additional information, might be:

Test statement:
James is taller than Paul, and Paul is taller than Alice.

Corresponding question:
Is Alice as tall as James?
Answer: No.

The particular feature to be noted about these two types of questions is that the former, because it requires additional information from the test taker, is asking for a judgement about perceived truth or falsity, whereas the second type of question, which is self-contained, is testing the ability of the test taker to make proper inferences from the information given and is not concerned about truth or falsity.

It can be seen, therefore, that the internal logic of these two types of question is quite different. The property that distinguishes them is the requirement of the first type that outside or personal information be supplied by the test taker. If such information is required, then the question is not about inferences, because people's knowledge, information and experience differ - and this will undoubtedly affect their answers. If, on the other hand, additional information is *not* required and the question is self-contained, then the question is purely about inferences of some kind and not about judgements of truth or falsity.

Clearly, anyone constructing a test, particularly a standardized test for general use, should be keenly aware of these crucial differences between test items. But this is precisely the confusion that contaminates the Watson–Glazer test and can be seen throughout the test in one form or another. It shows itself, for example, in the provision of test directions for self-contained questions, which would be appropriate for testing *inferences* and their validity, but the posing of questions that in fact require judgements about *truth* or *falsity* because they require further information. What I shall attempt to show, therefore, is that the questions are not really about what the authors claim in the directions, and that a student would do poorly if he or she followed the directions. In short, the rating of the real critical thinker would not be high on Watson–Glazer.

The first section of the test (which, incidentally, is the longest section) is described as being about 'inferences'. The section begins with specific directions, together with a sample question and correct answers to serve as a model. There are five detractors (that is, possible answers) for each question, and they are explained as follows (with the exception of that in the first paragraph, the emphasis is mine):

In this test, each exercise begins with a statement of facts which you are to regard as true. After each statement of facts you will find several possible inferences – that is, conclusions which some persons might make from the stated facts. Examine each inference separately, and make a decision as to its *degree* of truth or falsity [*sic*].

For each inference you will find spaces on the Answer Sheet labelled *T, PT, ID, PF,* and *F.* For each inference make a mark on the Answer Sheet under the appropriate label as follows:

T   if you think the inference is definitely TRUE; that it properly follows beyond a reasonable doubt *from the statement of facts given.*

PT if, *in the light of the facts given,* you think the inference is PROBABLY TRUE: that there is a better than even chance that it is true.

ID if you decide that there are INSUFFICIENT DATA, that you cannot tell *from the facts given* whether the inference is likely to be true or false; *if the facts provide no basis for judging one way or the other.*

PF if, *in the light of the facts given,* you think the inference is PROBABLY FALSE; that there is better than an even chance that it is false.

F   if you think the inference is definitely FALSE; that it is wrong, either because it misinterprets the *facts given,* or because it contradicts the facts or *necessary inferences from those facts.*

The italicized phrases in these directions clearly suggest that the questions are intended to be self-contained, since the answers are to be determined solely on the basis of the *given facts.* This, indeed, is as a true test for 'inferences' should be. However, this statement immediately follows these detailed instructions:

Sometimes, in deciding whether an inference is probably true or probably false, *you will have to use certain commonly accepted knowledge or information which practically every person has.*

Now the test taker learns, to his chagrin, that he must *not* decide solely on the given facts, as stated earlier, but must import some of his own 'common knowledge'. So, just in case the test taker is not thoroughly confused at this point, the directions proceed to offer an example.

EXAMPLE
Two hundred eighth-grade students voluntarily attended a recent week-end student forum conference in a Midwestern city. At this conference, the topics of race relations and means of achieving lasting world peace were discussed, since these were the problems the students selected as being most vital in today's world.

1.   As a group, the students who attended this conference showed a keener interest in humanitarian or broad social problems than have most eighth-grade students.
2.   The majority of these students were between the ages of 17 and 18.
3.   The students came from all sections of the country.
4.   The students discussed only labor relations problems.
5.   Some eighth-grade students felt that discussion of race relations and means of achieving world peace might be worthwhile.

Answers to Test 1

Inference

	T	PT	ID	PF	F
1	: :	■	: :	: :	: :
2	: :	: :	: :	■	: :
3	: :	: :	■	: :	: :
4	: :	: :	: :	: :	■
5	■	: :	: :	: :	: :

Being a model question, this example is naturally more straightforward than many of those which follow in the test itself. Even so, an explanatory discussion of this example follows:

> In the above example, inference 1 is probably true (PT) because (*as is common knowledge*) most eighth-grade students are not likely to show so much serious concern with broad social problems. It cannot be considered definitely true from the facts given because these facts provide no certain knowledge about the kind and degree of concern with world problems which other eighth-grade students might express. It is also possible that some of these students volunteered mainly because they wanted a week-end outing.
>
> Inference 2 is probably false (PF) because (*common knowledge*) there are relatively few eighth-grade students in the United States between 17 and 18 years of age.
>
> There is no evidence for inference 3. Thus there are insufficient data (ID) for making a judgement on the matter.
>
> Inference 4 is definitely false (F) because it is given in the statement of facts that ....[9]

It is clear from this discussion that, contrary to their original *directions*, Watson and Glazer expect the test taker to use his or her own 'general knowledge' to answer these questions. Thus what are described as self-contained questions (concerned with pure inference), are not in fact self-contained. Moreover, when one stops to consider the fact that many logic tests actually penalize students for reading into the question premises that are not given, it is clear that training in logic would be a disadvantage for such items. In the above example a student trained in logic would note that there is nothing actually stated or logically implied in the premises about students being keen or apathetic, nor is there anything about student ages. Thus he would feel constrained not to make any inferences about those questions. These items, however, demand that one forget logic, and use in its stead 'common knowledge'. But what, precisely, is 'common knowledge'? And to whom is it common? And should it always replace logic, or only in the Watson–Glazer test?

Students or test takers from the social sciences,

particularly those who studied statistics, would similarly be compelled to suppress all of their disciplinary training in answering these questions. Their training teaches them that one needs quantities of different data before one can justifiably make the sorts of generalization required by these answers. Indeed, for every question that is not a tautology or an overt contradiction (that is, *T* or *F*), a trained social scientist would have to mark *ID* because there are not sufficient data for any of these 'inferences'. In the first question, for example, the two hundred volunteer students might have been selected from tens of thousands of volunteers, many of whom might be even more keen than this particular group. The social scientist knows that such possibilities must be controlled, so that the issue is not prejudged by bias or opinion. Again, however, this type of disciplined thinking, critical thinking, must be suppressed.

In the section of the Watson–Glazer test entitled 'Interpretation' the same type of confusion is again manifest in slightly different form. We should ask: are the questions intended to be open (that is, do they require knowledge and information), or are they supposed to be self-contained? The directions to the test taker are anything but clear about this. They systematically require him to make a judgement about what is a reasonable belief (which suggests an open question) but at the same time restrict this judgement to information provided in a test paragraph (which suggests a self-contained question). The directions say (again, the emphasis is my own):

> For the purpose of this test assume that everything in the short paragraph is true. The problem is to judge whether or not each of the proposed conclusions *logically follows beyond a reasonable doubt from the information given in the paragraph.*
>
> If you think that the proposed conclusion follows beyond a reasonable doubt (even though it may not follow absolutely and necessarily), then make a heavy black mark between the appropriate dotted lines under the 'CONCLUSION FOL-LOWS' column on the Answer Sheet. If you think that the conclusion does *not* follow *beyond a reasonable doubt from the facts given*, then make a mark under 'CONCLUSION DOES NOT FOLLOW'.

The difficulty here lies, as it does for legal juries, in the meaning of the phrase 'beyond a reasonable doubt'. Precisely what, in general, is or is not 'beyond a reasonable doubt'? The answer to this question is partly a function of the personal knowledge, beliefs and experience of the individual making the judgement. That is, a person must bring to bear his own experience in making such an assessment.[10] Thus, from a logical or analytical point of view, the phrase 'beyond a reasonable doubt' renders the question an open one (that is, not self-contained). Yet, the directions conjoin this phrase with 'from the information provided in the paragraph', indicating that the question is intended to be self-contained. Thus, the directions to judge whether a conclusion 'logically follows beyond a reasonable doubt from the information given in the paragraph' is systematically ambiguous.

Many of the questions in this section require the test taker to make inferences about facts that are not expressly mentioned in the paragraph but might follow from the facts that are given. Thus the property of being expressly mentioned in the paragraph is not a necessary criterion for judging whether a conclusion does or does not follow. But what, then, is the necessary criterion on which to base such a judgement? Answer: what the test taker thinks is 'beyond a reasonable doubt'. However, this clearly involves the personal belief states of individual test takers. Consider this question from the test.

> Usually I fall asleep promptly, but about twice a month I drink coffee in the evening; and whenever I do, I lie awake and toss for hours after I go to bed.
> 74. My problem is mostly mental; I am overaware of the coffee when I drink it at night, anticipating that it will keep me awake, and therefore it does.
> 75. I don't fall asleep promptly after drinking coffee at night because the caffeine in coffee stimulates my nervous system for several hours after drinking it.
> 76. Whatever causes me to lie awake and toss at night is associated with my drinking coffee earlier in the evening.

When one remembers, from similar questions in this

section, that a putative fact *need not be mentioned in the paragraph*, one realizes that personal beliefs are required to judge what is 'reasonable' here. Someone might, therefore, justifiably regard any or none of these inferences as following 'beyond a reasonable doubt', depending on his or her beliefs. Watson and Glazer, however, have determined that only the last inference (76) 'logically follows beyond a reasonable doubt from the paragraph'. But we should notice that the paragraph does not say that coffee is associated with sleeplessness. This inference is only reasonable if one holds the empirical belief that coffee is (somehow) actually connected with sleeplessness. (An Aborigine or uninformed adolescent might not know of any such connection.) If one does not hold the empirical belief that coffee causes sleeplessness, then the first inference (74) might appear to be the most reasonable. The point is, however, that the contingent beliefs of individual test takers determine what will appear reasonable to each. Therefore these questions are not self-contained, as the directions indicate, and this seriously undermines their construct validity.

The last section of the test, 'The Evaluation of Arguments', is perhaps the clearest case of the confusion of self-contained questions with open ones. Here the test taker is asked to judge whether each of a series of arguments is individually 'strong' or 'weak'. The directions say that in order for an argument to be 'strong' it must be both important and directly related to the test question. If either of these conditions is not met, the argument is to be judged 'weak'.

Then, to suggest to the test taker that these questions are self-contained (require no outside opinions or information), the directions say:

> Judge each argument separately on its own merit; try not to let your personal attitude toward the question influence your evaluation.

But just before the actual questions begin the test taker is confronted with this last bit of advice:

> When the word 'should' is used as the first word in any of the

following questions, its meaning is 'Would the proposed action promote the general welfare of the people in the United States?'

This clearly involves the political views and value judgements of the individual test taker. Political liberals and conservatives might well disagree on every one of these items.[11] Moreover, what one considers important, which is one of the requirements of 'strong' argument, is similarly determined by one's value orientation. Thus even the basic criterion of 'strength' or 'weakness' is shot through with value considerations.

The following set of question and answers from this section illustrates these points:

> Should the United States government take over all the main industries in the country, employ all who want to work, and offer the products at cost price?
>> 9.5. No; so much concentration of economic and bureaucratic power in government would undermine our personal and political freedom.
>> 9.6. Yes; the government already operates post offices, highways, parks, military forces, public health services, and some other public services.
>> 9.7. No; the subsequent elimination of competition and the profit motive would result in much less initiative for production of useful new goods and services.

Which of these arguments is 'strong', in the sense of being 'important and directly related to the issue'? Whatever one's answer to this, it will clearly involve one's personal value judgements and political opinions. What appears 'strong' to some will appear 'weak' to others, depending on certain beliefs and attitudes. Thus it is not clear how one could possibly 'judge each argument separately on its own merit', as Watson and Glazer require, nor how one could prevent one's personal attitude toward the question from influencing an evaluation. The true critical thinker would find himself in an unceasing quandary when faced with such questions. The correct critical response would be to attack the questions, but (of course) there is no blank space for this.

So much for the construct and internal validity of the items themselves.

In order to support the validity and statistical reliability of the test (Forms YM and ZM), the accompanying manual presents normative data for eight different groups of test takers (ranging from grade 9 students through to college seniors), together with corresponding scores on nine other measures of mental abilities (ranging from IQ scores to College Entrance Exam Board results). These data are also intended to help potential test users for a number of other reasons, among which are the ability to make appropriate normative comparisons and to adjust their expectations for results accordingly.[12]

However, the normative data presented by Watson and Glazer permit alternative interpretations that would not support the validity of the test as a measure of critical thinking abilities. In particular, I draw attention to the very high correlation coefficients between IQ, reading ability and Watson–Glazer test results. The correlations with IQ range from 0.55 to 0.75 (Otis IQ), with a median of 0.68; and the correlations with reading ability range from 0.60 to 0.66, with a median of 0.64. Curiously, Watson and Glazer cite these high correlations as evidence for the validity of their test as a good measuring instrument for 'critical thinking ability'. In fact, however, these same correlations make a strong case that the test is measuring not so much critical thinking as IQ and/or reading ability. The onus is on Watson and Glazer to show that they have constructed a test for critical thinking as such; these data alone do not support that conclusion. It might be suggested, in fact, that these correlations are not higher because of the internal muddles of the Watson–Glazer test items themselves. The only direct evidence given by Watson and Glazer that their test is not simply a diluted IQ test is their statement:

> An examination of content of the various tests shows that the tasks imposed by the *Critical Thinking Appraisal* are quite different from those presented in commonly used intelligence measures.[13]

But this will not do, not only because it simply makes an unsubstantiated claim that the items appear different, but also because it goes nowhere towards showing that the skills required for the one test are in fact different from those required for the other.

With respect to the IQ correlation, they go on to conclude:

> It appears, therefore, that a high level of 'intelligence' as measured by conventional tests may be necessary, but not sufficient, for high attainment in critical thinking.

What is required, however, is to show that high IQ is not sufficient for high critical thinking ability. Without this proof, there are no data to suggest that it is a test of critical thinking and not IQ (albeit a deficient one).

A similar objection can be raised to the high correlation with reading ability. The test items, in fact, even look like items frequently found in reading comprehension tests. In this case, if a test taker understands the meaning of terms and phrases such as 'deductive', 'necessarily follows', 'conclusion does not follow', 'assumption' and the like, this comprehension provides an even greater advantage.

In order to show that the test is not a reading comprehension test (despite the high correlation) but is supposed to measure critical thinking ability *per se*, Watson and Glazer state:

> While it is true that a person must be able to read in order to perform effectively on the *Critical Thinking Appraisal*, the test items require mental activity more complicated than mere recognition of the vocabulary and comprehension of the sentences. Many persons who are superior readers, as measured by a reading test, may make relatively low scores on the *Critical Thinking Appraisal*. But if a person makes a relatively high score on the *Critical Thinking Appraisal*, he is also likely to score relatively high on a reading test.

The key sentence here is the one that claims that superior readers 'may make relatively low scores on the *Critical Thinking Appraisal*'. Certainly, it is logically possible that they *may* make low scores on the appraisal, but Watson's and Glazer's data do not show that this ever happens. On the contrary, their data show that the higher the reading ability, the higher the critical thinking scores. A much more crucial test would be to show that there are *in fact* people with high reading scores who do not score well on the appraisal, and that this is not due to chance. We might then have reason to believe that something other than reading comprehension is being measured by the test. Moreover, when Watson and Glazer compared the appraisal scores with a non-language test (the California Test of Mental Maturity Non-Language Test), which does not require reading comprehension, they got one of their lowest correlations, 0.43. Thus the available evidence suggests that the variance on Watson and Glazer scores is accounted for by reading comprehension. And there is no statistical evidence that suggests that an independent or unique set of skills, called critical thinking, is being measured.

The Cornell Critical Thinking Tests

The widespread popularity of the Watson–Glazer test is presently being challenged by the increasing use of another set of tests, the Cornell Critical Thinking Tests. The Cornell Critical Thinking Tests appear in two forms: 'Level X', which is recommended for children grades 7 through 12, and 'Level Z', which is more difficult and is recommended for college-aged students. The authors of both these tests are Robert H. Ennis and Jason Millman.

In general, the Cornell tests represent an improvement over the Watson–Glazer test in at least two respects. First, the directions are clear and straightforward, and the tasks involved are a direct manifestation of the instructions. Second, the authors appear to recognize the difference between 'self-contained questions' and 'open' (or divergent) questions and do not confuse the two. In each form of the test there is one section that asks 'open' questions, but the reasons for this are quite different from those of Watson and Glazer. Watson and Glazer confuse the distinction between truth and validity, which vitiates the 'self-contained' nature of their questions, whereas the 'open' questions of the Cornell tests stem from the operative conception of critical thinking contained therein. It is, in fact, Robert Ennis's concept of critical thinking, which was discussed in chapter 3.[14] According to this concept of critical thinking, it will be recalled, there are twelve 'aspects' (or abilities) and three 'dimensional criteria', many of which require the thinker to go beyond the data given and to make assessments of statements based on certain far-reaching criteria. It is not surprising, therefore, that as an author of the Cornell tests Ennis should have included some items of this type.

The major shortcoming of both the Cornell tests is that the format of a standardized multiple-choice test does not permit the comprehensive or circumspect judgements that are required by the concept of critical thinking. The short questions, with their even shorter answers, prohibit the use of Ennis's 'dimensional criteria' (particularly the 'pragmatic dimension'), which, as he argues, is fundamental to the 'correct assessing of statements'. The resulting content of the questions is thus indistinguishable from what might be found in any beginning-logic test. These tests would be much more aptly titled 'The Cornell Informal Logic Tests', and, like other tests of informal logic, they suffer from the lack of precision that is endemic in that subject area.

Several sections of each of the Cornell tests, it must be admitted, are free of ambiguity and have precise, correct answers among the 'detractors'. But these are the sections that test for formal, deductive inferences, whose precision is determined by the nature of that subject matter and is not a peculiar characteristic of critical thinking as such. When the questions turn from deductive inferences to questions requiring judgements that are more characteristic of critical thinking (for example, those that involve several of Ennis's twelve 'aspects' in conjunction with the 'dimensional criteria') the items become problematic, in that they admit of more than one correct answer. For example, the 'Level X' Cornell test has twenty-three items on inductive reasoning for which equally strong arguments can be made for answers contrary to the keyed responses. As a result, justifiable answers are routinely penalized on these items, and the test is considerably weakened in consequence. Valid questions requiring inductive reasoning are difficult to construct in the best of circumstances because no matter how much information is provided, it is usually possible to interpret those data in several reasonable patterns. Moreover, a standardized multiple-choice test is a particularly inept vehicle for posing such questions.

Why, then, we might ask, should the authors of the Cornell test include such troublesome items? The answer to this question is to be found in their operative conception of critical thinking, which reveals itself here in two parts. First, they correctly believe that critical thinking consists of more than deductive reasoning and should somehow test the capacity for rational judgement in broader contexts – hence the section on inductive reasoning. Second they believe – incorrectly, as I have shown – that inductive reasoning, like critical thinking, is a generalized skill that transfers across any subject matter.

The 'Level Z' form of the Cornell test also has a large section of questions on inductive reasoning, and happily the keyed answers are not nearly as contentious as those on the 'X' form. However, the reasons for this do nothing to save the items as valid questions requiring critical thinking. There is so much information provided in the test paragraph, and the level of 'inference' required is so low, that they are clearly questions of reading comprehension more than anything else. In the few cases where the information is not provided in the paragraph the keyed answers are correspondingly as contentious as they were in the 'X' form of the test.

In addition, Section II of the 'Z' form of the test, which alone contains over 20 per cent of the questions, consists of items that *cannot* have definitive answers. Again, these questions stem from Ennis's concept of critical thinking, which includes such things as 'picking out ambiguity in a line of reasoning', 'grasping the meaning of a statement' and so on – all of which are variations of the informal fallacies. Indeed, the underlying difficulty with this section of questions is precisely that of the informal fallacies generally. These difficulties were, we recall, that there is no definitive way in which to establish that a fallacy as such has in fact been committed; that there are no objective criteria for rank-ordering the seriousness of the different fallacies; and that a given statement or argument can commit more than one fallacy at the same time. This section of the 'Z' test asks the test taker to read a short discussion and then to 'pick out the one best reason why some of this thinking is faulty.' However, public criteria for establishing 'the one best reason' are not forthcoming, just as they are not for the informal fallacies. Consider a random example taken from this section:

> 12.   DOBERT: I guess you know that to put chlorine in the water is to threaten the health of everyone of Gallton's citizens, and that, you'll admit, is bad.
> ALGAN: What right do you have to say that our health will be threatened?
> DOBERT: 'Healthy living' may be defined as living according to nature. Now we don't find chlorine added to water in nature. Therefore, everyone's health would be threatened if chlorine were added.
> PICK OUT THE ONE BEST REASON WHY SOME OF THIS THINKING IS FAULTY.
> A.   Dobert is using emotional language which doesn't help to make his argument reasonable.
> B.   Dobert's thinking is in error.
> C.   Dobert is using a word in two different ways.

If one restricts oneself to the information provided in this question (as the instructions prescribe), any of the following interpretations could be justifiably defended: (1) that all of the above errors are committed; (2) that none of the above errors is necessarily committed; (3) that there are not sufficient data provided to establish any single error as more serious than the others. The point is that the question itself is 'faulty' because there are no definitive criteria for establishing the 'best reason' from this information.

One might argue, for example, that Dobert is using

'emotional language' in discussing a problem that requires calm analysis by his continued references to chlorine's 'threat' to everyone's health. One could conclude also that Dobert's thinking is in error because it does not follow that the addition of chlorine to water (in proper amounts) will result in damaged health. And one could note that Dobert is using the word 'health' in two different ways – first, in the sense of 'free from disease', and second, in the sense of 'living close to Mother Nature'. Conversely, the negations of these might be defended as follows. One might argue that Dobert's use of 'emotional language' is not excessive but appropriate to the seriousness of the consequences at stake. One could claim that Dobert is implying not that there is a logical connection between adding chlorine to drinking water and damage to health, but rather that there is a contingent connection between them. And one might infer that Dobert is not using the word 'health' in two different ways, but only appears to do so – in fact, he could be using it in the sense of 'living close to Mother Nature' all through the discussion. Which set of these interpretations is correct? And how are we to decide on the basis of the limited information given? More important, however, is how is the test taker to determine which one of these six possibilities is 'best'? Where there are no objective criteria, there can be no objective assessment.

Another upsetting feature of the answers in this section is that over half of the questions have 'detractors' that say, 'Dobert's thinking is in error' or 'There is an error in thinking in this part' when the directions explicitly state: *'the thinking in each question is faulty.'* Thus this type of 'detractor' is always tautologically correct. Could any answer be stronger than that? And does this, in effect, reduce the number of real 'detractors' to two?

In sum, the Cornell Thinking Tests (Forms X and Z) are only slightly better than the Watson–Glazer tests as measures of critical thinking. The authors have not confused truth with validity (as did Watson and Glazer), and they have tried to test for rational judgements that go beyond the 'deductive inferences' that are so common in most tests. But this latter point is precisely where the tests go awry because rational judgement of a non-deductive sort is not restricted to a unique set of rules, nor to singular solutions. This type of difficulty is an inevitable consequence of construing critical thinking as a generalized skill whose parts are all standardized like autos on an assembly line. In this case, however, the alleged parts are too varied and too complex to be captured validly in a standardized test.

As suggested earlier when discussing reading, the notions of literacy and reading comprehension are too complex to be reduced to a few decoding skills. Similarly, critical thinking defies this type of reductionism with the same dire consequences. Both areas of research proceed from the same false premise: that their respective processes are simple collections of more or less mechanical skills.

I believe it is possible to test for *bona fide* critical thinking in a number of ways, but any such test should at least meet the following conditions:

1   That the test be subject-specific in an area (or areas) of the test taker's experience or preparation. This is required because knowledge and information are necessary ingredients of critical thinking.
2   That the answer format permit more than one justifiable answer. Thus an essay might better fit the task, awkward and time-consuming as this might be. (This recognizes that there is usually more than one good way to pluck a goose.)
3   That good answers are not predicated on being *right*, in the sense of true, but on the *quality of the justification given* for a response.
4   That the test results should not be used as a measure of one's capacity or innate ability, but as a learned accomplishment – which is usually the result of specific training or experience.

Actually, tests found in normal discipline (or subject) related courses, when sensibly set, come far closer to meeting these requirements than any standardized test available on the market. And it is a *market*!

NOTES

1. Several excellent anthologies are available that provide introductions to this literature. Among them are: F. B. Murray and J. J. Pikulski (eds.), *The Acquisition of Reading* (Baltimore: University Park, 1978); Doris V. Gunderson (ed.), *Language and Reading: An Interdisciplinary Approach* (Washington, D.C.: Center for Applied Linguistics, 1970); K. S. Goodman and J. T. Fleming (eds.), *Psycholinguistics and the Teaching of Reading* (Delaware: International Reading, 1968); John P. De Cecco (ed.), *The Psychology of Language, Thought and Instruction* (San Francisco: Holt, Rinehart & Winston, 1968).

2. This group would include writers such as Thomas G. Sticht, George A. Miller, Morton Wiener and Ward Cromer, to name just a few. Relevant papers by these writers can be found in Murray and Pikulski, *The Acquisition of Reading*, and in Gunderson, *Language and Reading*.

3. 'Reading and reading difficulty: a conceptual analysis', *Harvard Educational Review*, vol. 37, no. 4 (Fall, 1967), pp. 620–43.

4. See, for example, R. L. Venesky, R. C. Calfee and R. S. Chapman, 'Skills required for learning to read', in Gunderson, *Language and Reading*, pp. 36–54.

5. 'The acquisition of literacy by children and adults', in Murray and Pikulski, *The Acquisition of Reading*, pp. 131–62.

6. *ibid.*, p. 132.

7. For a list of these studies, see O. Buros (ed.), *The Seventh Mental Measurements Yearbook* (Highland Park, N.J.: Gryphon Press, 1972), p. 783.

8. *Watson–Glazer Critical Thinking Appraisal Manual, Forms YM and ZM* (New York: Harcourt Brace, Jovanovich, 1964), p. 2. An even more awkward locution appears on p. 8 of the test itself, which says: '*For the purposes of this test you are to regard each argument as true*' (their italics)! Again, arguments are not 'true'.

9. *ibid.*, p. 2.

10. This is not to suggest that what is ultimately reasonable is a matter of personal opinion (that is, relative), but only to point out that individual perceptions can and do differ on such things.

11. This criticism was also made of this type of item by Robert Ennis, in 'An appraisal of the Watson–Glazer Critical Thinking Appraisal', *Journal of Educational Research*, vol. 52, no. 4 (December, 1958), pp. 155–8.

12. Several reviews of the psychometric data associated with Watson–Glazer can be found in the literature. See Buros, *The Seventh Mental Measurements Yearbook*, pp. 1214–5; see also Bruce L. Stewart, 'Testing for critical thinking: a review of the resources', in R. H.

Ennis (ed.), *Rational Thinking Reports Number 2* (Urbana, Ill., 1979), which contains clear and concise reviews of twenty-four other critical thinking tests as well.

13. Test manual, p. 10.
14. See 'A concept of critical thinking', *Harvard Educational Review*, vol. 32, no. 1, (Winter, 1962), pp. 83–111.

CHAPTER 7

Forward to Basics

It was argued in chapter 1 that critical thinking can be described as the propensity and skill to engage in an activity with reflective scepticism. This might have seemed at the time to be far too simple a solution to an even simpler problem, but subsequent chapters have shown in how many and often diverse ways the concept of critical thinking has been first misconstrued and then used as a basis for various teaching programmes and standardized tests. We are now in a position to appreciate the importance of being clear about the meaning of critical thinking, a meaning that should not be lost in the process of trying to teach or test for it. The logic of the concept, as it were, precludes some procedures and permits others. What are some of the more practical consequences that can be inferred from this analysis?

Knowing what critical thinking is in itself says nothing about whether it should or should not be introduced into a school system. Indeed, even knowing that the concept of education logically entails critical thinking (see chapter 2) implies nothing about its required place in our schools, because there is nothing in the logic of education that requires that schools should engage in education. There is nothing contradictory in saying, 'This is a fine school system, and I recommend it to others, even though it does not engage in education.' Logically, all that is required of a well managed school is that directed learning *of some kind* take place in it. We should not lose sight of the fact that a society's decision to have its schools engage in education is a public policy decision that reflects priorities and values and can differ between and among societies. Indeed, it could be argued that many of the development problems of Third World countries are directly linked to school systems that have prematurely emphasized education at the expense of training in basic vocational skills. Latin, literature and geometry might get one into Cambridge, but they do not put food on tables or fix tractors. The specific purpose of a given school is determined by policy not logic. All we can say is that if education is a goal of schooling, then critical thinking must be included as part of that goal.

In professional, vocational or training institutions the role of critical thinking is at most contingently connected with these things. There is no logical relation between learning to do a job or to perform a specific service and critical thinking. But since any procedure or performance is in principle open to improvement, institutions that teach these tasks could greatly benefit by including critical thinking in their curriculum. Moreover, the analysis of critical thinking presented here has attempted to stress that any activity requiring deliberation is capable of employing critical thinking, and that it is not restricted to propositional knowledge, as others have implied. Indeed, even courses in consumerism or how-to-do-it courses might well find an important role for critical thinking because even these areas have a quasi-epistemic foundation that is subject to scrutiny. (However, the specific character and content of critical thinking will be different in each area, since it is not an isolatable set of unique skills.)

It has not been the purpose of this essay to establish curriculum objectives for our schools. That, again, is a matter not of logic but of social policy, which requires argument of its own. Rather, the primary task here has been to clarify the nature of critical thinking for any context where it is of interest or concern. We may ask, however, where is it of interest and concern? If we restrict ourselves to present-day, English-speaking schools, we are likely to get a fairly blurred picture of the role of critical thinking. On the one hand, there is widespread public dissatisfaction with students who either cannot or will not think for themselves, even about subjects in the curriculum. Yet, on the other hand, there is a constant cry to move 'back to basics' at almost every level. At first blush, these two objectives appear to be pulling in opposite directions. To get students thinking for themselves, after all, would require curricula and teaching techniques more sophisticated than any we have thus far been able to mass-produce. The 'back to basics' movement, however, appears to be a call for a no-frills emphasis on basic information and skills. Can both of these objectives be attained? And if so, how?

I suggest that these apparently conflicting objectives or trends could be reconciled by being very clear about what critical thinking is and how it contributes to a basic understanding of subject matter of various kinds.

What is of value in the view of the 'back to basic' movement is the idea that there is, after all, something fundamentally important in traditional academic learning and that it is not a mere cultural appendage. However, the traditional methods of schooling have always been, and continue to be, seriously deficient in promoting independent, productive thought. By default, as it were, critical independent thought has been treated as an innate *capacity* rather than a variety of *learned abilities* and has thus been left to the student's native intelligence or to chance.[1]

There are three distinct questions that can be posed to the 'back to basics' movement:

1   What subjects constitute so-called basic subjects?
2   What kind of understanding, within a subject, constitutes a basic understanding?
3   What methods are most conducive to imparting this basic understanding?

An analysis of critical thinking, as such, can do little towards answering the first question, and I do not here propose to enter that debate. Critical thinking can be employed in any subject requiring deliberation. With respect to the two remaining questions, however, the analysis of epistemology and of critical thinking presented here can offer some very powerful suggestions merely by integrating the key features of critical thinking in an intelligent way. This purpose may best be served by summarizing what these features are and how they are related to one another.

In chapter 2 it was argued that epistemology is, in effect, the analysis of good reasons for belief, including their specific character and foundation. Also, because collective human experience has discovered that different kinds of beliefs often have different kinds of good reason supporting them, it follows that there will be many different epistemologies corresponding to different fields of human endeavour. A corollary of this is that logic itself is parasitic upon epistemology, since logic is merely the formalization of good reasons once they have been discovered. Thus epistemology, and to some extent logic, have intra-field validity but not necessarily inter-field validity (see chapter 2). (Most programmes for critical thinking effectively deny this proposition, hence my disagreement with them.) These reflections on epistemology can provide us with some important insights into the nature of critical thinking itself.

Assuming that my analysis of critical thinking is roughly correct, we can begin to see what the ingredients of the skills involved might be. Like most skills, reflective scepticism minimally requires knowledge of the field in question; in particular, it requires knowledge of the epistemic foundations of that field. Epistemology, conveniently, is none other than the study of the foundations of various types of belief. It is reasonable to assume that in order for one's scepticism to be intelligently employed (hence reflective), one should know something about the epistemology of the field in question. Such knowledge would not only enable one to detect various misapplications of logic itself, but would also help to move the locus of belief from authority and hearsay to the rational foundations of the various kinds of knowledge itself. In short, the epistemology of various fields, more than anything else, provides one with the requisite knowledge to employ his critical acumen effectively. When a person knows how to suspend judgement for the purpose of using his epistemic understanding of an issue, and does in fact do so, we say of that person that he is a critical thinker. Thus, the core ingredient of critical thinking is foundational knowledge – which is epistemology.

It was further argued that since the various fields of human endeavour are vastly different and have epistemologies (and sometimes logics) corresponding to them, it is not surprising that critical thinking is not a generalized skill. Even a Renaissance man, competent in all fields, would possess many different sets of skills, not one set that he applied to all fields. Critical thinking skills, like others, similarly differ according to subject matter. A person might have the disposition to think critically in all areas, in the sense that he tries to do this, but he is not in fact a critical thinker unless he has an understanding of the area or field in which he is being critical. This is because critical thinking is tied more closely to specific knowledge and understanding than to any specific set of allegedly transferable skills. (This view, too, contradicts the received opinion about critical thinking.)

Contemporary programmes in critical thinking attempt to bypass the problem of having knowledge of a field by treating the requisite knowledge as though it were common knowledge. But where there is only common knowledge, there can only be common criticism – which is usually plain enough for one and all to see. This view not only represents a very shallow, or superficial, understanding of the cognitive ingredients of critical thinking, but it is also forced to underestimate and play down the real complexities that usually underlie even apparently 'common' or 'everyday' problems. The solutions to 'common', 'everyday' problems, if they are in fact problems, are seldom common or everyday. In any event, the educational aspirations of our schools are (fortunately) set higher than the treatment of issues that could otherwise be solved by common sense. Where common sense can solve a problem, there is hardly a need for special courses in critical thinking. And where common sense cannot solve a problem, one quickly finds the need for subject-specific information; hence, the traditional justification for subject-oriented courses.

It is all too common, however, for specific subject-oriented courses to permit information and authority to rule in the place of reason, and where authority reigns unreflective obedience will follow. Critical thinking, by contrast, requires knowledge of the reasons that lie behind the putative facts and various voices of authority. Without such knowledge, even someone who is disposed to think critically has no real basis for the suspension of his belief and thus no grounds for forming an opinion of his own. An epistemological orientation towards the teaching of various subjects is one that can provide those reasons, since epistemology is none other than the analysis and study of the various kinds of good reason for belief.

If there is a genuine interest in promoting critical thinking in our schools, therefore, I would envisage courses that included the epistemology of a subject as an integral part of that subject. In a very real sense, approaching subjects in this way might be seen as moving *forward to basics*. It would be moving *forward* in the sense that our conception of what it would mean to teach a subject would change to include its epistemology as a fundamental component. And it would be teaching *basics* in the sense that there is no understanding more basic than that which epistemology provides. In an epistemological approach to subjects the rationale and justification for various beliefs, statements and methods of procedure are every bit as important as the putative facts and procedures themselves. A student would learn not only what is thought to be the case in a given field (that is, the 'facts') but also why it is so regarded. With this kind of understanding (that is, seeing the facts in both their most persuasive and most vulnerable lights), a person is then in a position to make the kinds of judgement required of a critical thinker.

The appropriate inclusion of epistemology in school subjects raises many more questions than can be adequately dealt with here, not the least of which would involve the appropriate methods for preparing teachers to present subjects in this way. As a first step, my inclination would be to have curriculum specialists from specific fields join forces with epistemologists who have an interest in those fields in order to develop epistemologically oriented curricula for specific subjects and also to develop appropriate training methods for teachers. In some cases this might simply involve recasting familiar materials into an epistemological framework, while in others it might involve the development of entirely new materials. In all cases, however, the epistemic foundations of various facts, beliefs and methods of procedure would be systemically included as an integral part of the subject; and test questions would be designed to see that understanding of them had been achieved. In short, the epistemology of a subject would not be simply an additional aspect to be studied when time and convenience permit, but a central framework around which the subject is built.

It may well be that certain segments of the public would react adversely to such a curriculum, since it would to some extent replace the dominance of facts and skills by an emphasis on understanding their justification. Obviously, there must be some trade-offs. But such an adverse reaction, it seems to me, would be tantamount to reneging on a commitment to critical thinking. One cannot have one's cake and eat it. I put the case very simply, therefore: if a community is genuinely interested in the development of critical thinking in students, then these are the sorts of change it is most reasonable to introduce.

Putting aside, for the moment, complex questions of specific curricula and training procedures, there are some perennial questions about critical thinking that can now be answered more directly. First, writers such as Edward de Bono, Robert Ennis and others have frequently raised the question of whether critical thinking might best be taught as a separate subject, as opposed to integrating it with other subjects. The analysis of critical thinking provided here makes it abundantly clear that it can only be taught as part of a specific subject and never in isolation. Indeed, the very idea of teaching critical thinking in isolation from specific content is incoherent. Those programmes that attempt to use 'common knowledge' as the content of critical thinking are forced to settle for superficial treatments of complex questions. Moreover, the type of skill that might be acquired through the so-called 'logic approach' to critical thinking (for example, the recognition of fallacies) would be developed in a more meaningful way as a by-product of the epistemological approach to subjects. Properly trained physicists, historians, and art critics are as quick to recognize fallacious reasoning as anyone trained in informal logic – even though they might not be able to name the fallacy. And in their fields, moreover, they are even better at detecting weak reasoning. There is no defensible justification for constructing courses in reasoning and critical thinking in isolation from specific subject areas.

A second perennial question about critical thinking, which has recently been discussed by Bryce Hudgins[2] and by Matthew Lipman, Ann M. Sharp and Frederick Oscanyan,[3] has to do with the age or grade level at which critical thinking should be introduced. Should critical thinking be introduced at the primary level? Or should it perhaps wait until secondary school? Hudgins, and to a lesser extent Lipman *et al.*, construe this question as a developmental question; that is, they want to know, as does Piaget, the age at which children are intellectually capable of thinking critically. Then, they go on to argue, since their research indicates that young children are in fact capable of critical thinking, at least in its rudimentary form, we ought to introduce it as early as possible. Indeed, Lipman *et al.* have been develolping materials for just this purpose.[4]

But surely the developmental question about cognitive capability is but half of what is at issue in such curriculum decisions? From the mere fact that young children are capable of handling certain types of material it does not follow that they *ought* to engage in such activity. Children, after all, are capable of many things that better judgement often suggests postponing. Despite claims by Lipman *et al.* that the introduction of primary school philosophy has improved pupils' general reading skills, one should view such results with caution. In addition to a wide range of overlap between what is directly taught and what is subsequently tested in such studies, which renders the results unsurprising, a recent study in Oregon showed that specific training in penmanship improved student's overall grade averages.[5] In the face of such claims, it is not clear what schools should do. What is clear, however, is that answers to questions about what children can do, and in fact do, in certain circumstances will not by themselves answer questions about what we ought to have them do.

As to when it is reasonable to introduce critical thinking into curricula, we can get some guidance from the nature of critical thinking itself. For example, since one of the preconditions of critical thinking is that one should possess knowledge and information about (or within) a given field, it follows that some time must first be spent on providing that basic information. One cannot think critically about X until one knows something about X. Experience has taught us, moreover, that elementary schools are fully occupied with their efforts to impart the three Rs, together with the most elementary information about the world around them. (Indeed, some critics contend that they do not manage even this very well.) The elementary schools are, in short, fully and properly engaged in attempting to provide students with the prerequisites of critical thinking. For all these reasons, then, I would not recommend trying to introduce critical thinking into elementary school curricula, even though it might be possible, in some sense, to do so. The schools simply have too much to do already. And if we can accomplish these basic achievements with some success, we are then in an excellent position to begin developing critical thinking in a more meaningful way at some later stage.

I. A. Snook has also raised a question in 'Teaching pupils to think'[6] to which my analysis of critical thinking can directly speak. It has to do with the kinds of subject or school programme that best promote independent thinking by students. Snook criticizes the so-called 'disciplines approach', usually associated with R. S. Peters and Paul Hirst, on the grounds that it teaches not so much independent thinking as 'academic' thinking, which, he claims, is out of touch with day-to-day problems. Snook also criticizes the 'inquiry' or 'problem-solving' approach, usually associated with John Dewey, on the grounds that it pays too little attention to differences in knowledge and skill that distinguish different types of problem. Snook says of Dewey:

> In his advocacy of problem-solving he tended to confuse logic and psychology, and overlooked the specificity of problems: the lawyer, the physicist, and the carpenter solve problems, but there is little in common between what they do to solve them.[7]

In the present book one might detect a certain bias toward the so-called 'disciplines approach'; this is perhaps true, but nothing I have to say about critical thinking depends upon this bias. Indeed, as I see it, one of the strengths of the present analysis is that while it recognizes that critical thinking is connected logically with specific tasks or subject matter, it places no *a priori* restrictions on what that subject matter may be. Critical thinking could well play a substantial role in courses on consumerism, business management or how-to-do-it, just as it can in the more traditional disciplines. I have attempted to emphasize that critical thinking is not restricted to propositional knowledge, as most of my predecessors have implied. Moreover, it is crucial to recognize that the specific ingredients of critical thinking will differ according to task or subject, and that it comprises neither any specific set of skills nor 'logical' skills: nothing that has been said should disquiet Professor Snook. However, I would not extol the virtues of so-called 'common-sense' or 'day-to-day' knowledge as much as Snook does, because few problems worthy of our systematic attention are amenable to obvious solutions. So-called 'common sense' is often mutually shared ignorance. Research, study and effort still appear to be our strongest suit against such ignorance.

Finally, I should be the first to point out that my analysis states explicitly that critical thinking consists in both a disposition and a skill, and that I have said virtually nothing about the dispositional aspects of critical thinking (that is, what makes people want to use the skill once they have it). The reasons for this omission are twofold. First, among philosophers, psychologists and educators there has been sufficient confusion over the meaning of critical thinking, and particularly over the nature of the skills involved, to warrant special treatment of this topic. Second, the question of how best to inculcate the disposition or propensity to use one's critical skills involves many more empirical questions than I, as a philosopher, have the specific knowledge to treat. No doubt the question still has many unresolved and untested dimensions. I will say, however, that whatever the final verdict about these issues, I would be greatly surprised if it involved teachers who were not themselves critical thinkers.

NOTES

1. On this point I concur with Ennis, D'Angelo, Scriven and de Bono, all of whom believe that productive thinking can be taught and learned.
2. *Learning and Thinking* (Itasca, Ill.: F. E. Peacock, 1978), pp. 179–80.
3. *Philosophy in the Classroom* (West Caldwell, N.J.: 1977).
4. See, for example, *Harry Stottlemeier's Discovery* (N.J.: IPAC, 1974) and *Lisa* (N.J.: Universal Diversified Services, 1976).
5. Reported in *Time* magazine, 28 January 1980, p. 43.
6. *Studies in Philosophy and Education*, vol. 8, no. 3 (Winter, 1974), pp. 146–62.
7. *ibid.*, p. 158.

Bibliography

Annis, David B., *Techniques of Critical Reasoning* (Columbus, Ohio: Charles E. Merrill, 1974)

Bakan, David, *On Method: Toward a Reconstruction of Psychological Investigation* (San Francisco: Jossey-Bass, 1968)

Barrow, Robin, *Common Sense and the Curriculum* (London: George Allen & Unwin, 1976)

Bloom, B. S. (ed.), *Taxonomy of Educational Objectives: The Classification of Educational Goals, Handbook 1: The Cognitive Domain* (New York: David McKay, 1956)

Buros, Oscar (ed.), *The Seventh Mental Measurements Yearbook* (Highland Park, N.J. : Gryphon Press, 1972)

Capaldi, Nicholas, *The Art of Deception*, 2nd ed. (New York: Prometheus Books, 1975)

Churchman, C. West and Buchanon, Bruce G., 'On the design of inductive systems: some philosophical problems', *British Journal of Philosophy of Science*, vol. 20 (1969), pp. 311–23

Cohen, M. and Nagel, E., *Introduction to Logic and Scientific Method* (New York: Harcourt, Brace & World, 1934)

D'Angelo, Edward, *The Teaching of Critical Thinking* (Amsterdam: B. R. Gruner, 1971)

de Bono, Edward, *The Five-Day Course in Thinking* (New York: Basic Books, 1967)

de Bono, Edward, *The Dog Exercising Machine* (New York: S & S, 1971)

de Bono, Edward, *The Mechanism of Mind* (Harmondsworth: Penguin, 1971)

de Bono, Edward, *The Use of Lateral Thinking* (Harmondsworth: Penguin, 1971)

de Bono, Edward, *Lateral Thinking for Management* (New York: McGraw-Hill, 1971)

de Bono, Edward, *Children Solve Problems* (Harmondsworth: Penguin, 1972)

de Bono, Edward, *PO: Beyond Yes and No* (Harmondsworth: Penguin, 1973)

de Bono, Edward, 'But how do you teach thinking?', *Times Educational Supplement*, 17 August 1973, p. 4

de Bono, Edward, *CoRT Thinking Lesson* (Blandford Forum, Dorset: Direct Educational Services, 1974)

de Bono, Edward, *Thinking Course for Juniors* (Blandford Forum, Dorset: Direct Educational Services, 1974) de Bono, Edward, *Teaching Thinking* (London: Maurice Temple Smith, 1976)

de Bono, Edward, *Lateral Thinking: A Textbook of Creativity* (Harmondsworth: Penguin, 1977)

De Cecco, John P. (ed.), *The Psychology of Language, Thought and Instruction* (San Francisco: Holt, Rinehart & Winston, 1968)

DeMorgan, Augustus, *Formal Logic* (London: Taylor & Walton, 1847)

Empiricus, Sextus, 'Against the logicians', *Works*, vol. 2

Ennis, Robert, 'An appraisal of the Watson–Glazer Critical Thinking Appraisal', *Journal of Educational Research*, vol. 52, no. 4 (December, 1958), pp. 155–8

Ennis, H. Robert, 'A concept of critical thinking', *Harvard Educational Review*, vol. 32, no. 1 (Winter, 1962), pp. 83–111

Ennis, Robert, 'Notes for "a conception of rational thinking"', *Proceedings of the American Philosophy of Education Society*, 1979

Fearnside, W. Ward, and Holther, William B., *Fallacy: The Counterfeit of Argument* (Englewood Cliffs, N.J.: Prentice-Hall, 1959)

Feigenbaum, E., and Feldman, J. (eds.), *Computers and Thought* (New York: McGraw-Hill, 1963)

Gilbert, Michael A., *How to Win an Argument* (New York: McGraw-Hill, 1980)

Goodman, K. S., and Fleming, J. T. (eds.), *Psycholinguistics and the Teaching of Reading* (Delaware: International Reading, 1968)

Gunderson, Doris V. (ed.), *Language and Reading: An Interdisciplinary Approach* (Washington, D.C.: Center for Applied Linguistics, 1970)

Hamblin, C. L. *Fallacies* (London: Methuen, 1970)

Hudgins, Bryce B., *Learning and Thinking* (Itasca, Ill.: F. E. Peacock, 1978)

Johnson, Ralph H., and Blair, J. Anthony, 'The recent development of informal logic', *Informal Logic: The First International Symposium* (San Francisco: Edgepress, 1980)

Johnson, R. H., and Blair, A. J., *Logical Self-Defence* (New York: McGraw-Hill, 1980)

Joseph, H. W. B., *An Introduction to Logic* (Oxford: Clarendon Press, 1916)

Kaplan, Abraham, *The Conduct of Inquiry* (San Francisco: Chandler, 1964)

Kleinmuntz, B. (ed.), *Problem Solving: Research, Method and Theory* (New York: Krieger, 1965)

Lipman, Matthew, *Harry Stottlemeier's Discovery* (West Caldwell, N.J.: IAPC, 1974)

Lipman, Matthew, *Lisa* (West Caldwell, N.J.: Universal Diversified Services, 1976)

Lipman, Matthew, Sharp, Ann M., and Oscanyan, Frederick, *Philosophy in the Classroom* (West Caldwell, N.J.: IAPC, 1977)

Martin, Jane Roland, 'On the reduction of "knowing that" to "knowing how"', in B. O. Smith and R. H. Ennis (eds.), *Language and Concepts in Education* (Chicago: Rand McNally, 1961)

Martin, Jane Roland, *Explaining, Understanding and Teaching* (New York: McGraw-Hill, 1970)

McPeck, John E., 'The context of discovery in context', *Proceeding of XV*

World Congress of Philosophy, Book III (Varna, Bulgaria: Sofia Press Production Centre, 1973)

McPeck, John E., 'A logic of discovery: lessons from history and current prospects', *Dissertation Abstracts* (Ann Arbor, Michigan: University of Michigan Microfilms, 1973)

Minsky, Marvin L., 'Some methods of artificial intelligence and heuristic programming', *Mechanization of Thought Processes*, National Physical Laboratory Symposium, vol. 1 (London: HMSO, 1959), pp. 5–27

Murray, F. B., and Pikulski, J. J. (eds.), *The Acquisition of Reading* (Baltimore: University Park, 1978)

Newell, A., 'Heuristic programming: ill-structured problems', in *Progress in Operations Research* (in press)

Newell, A., Shaw, J., and Simon, H., *Elements of a Theory of Human Problem Solving*, Paper P-971 (Santa Monica: Rand Corporation, 1957)

'Nowadays, Writing is Off the Wall', *Time* magazine, 28 January 1980, p. 43

Passmore, John, 'On teaching to be critical', in R. S. Peters (ed.), *The Concept of Education* (London: Routledge and Kegan Paul, 1967), p. 193

Perelman, C., and Olbrechts-Tyteca, L., *The New Rhetoric: A Treatise on Argumentation* (South Bend, Ind.: University of Notre Dame, 1969)

Peters, R. S., 'On teaching to be critical', in R. S. Peters (ed.), *The Concept of Education* (London: Routledge & Kegan Paul, 1973)

Polanyi, Michael, *Personal Knowledge: Towards a Post-Critical Philosophy* (New York: Harper & Row, 1962)

Popper, Karl, *The Logic of Scientific Discovery* (New York: Harper & Row, 1968)

Quine, W. V. O., 'Two dogmas of empiricism' in *From a Logical Point of View* (New York: Harper & Row, 1963)

Reichenbach, Hans, *Experience and Prediction* (Chicago: University of Chicago Press, 1938)

Richards, I. A., *The Meaning of Meaning* (New York: Harcourt, Brace, 1956)

Ryle, Gilbert, 'A puzzling element in the notion of thinking', in P. F. Strawson (ed.), *Studies in the Philosophy of Thought and Action* (New York: Oxford University Press, 1968)

Scheffler, Israel, *The Conditions of Knowledge* (Glenview, Ill.: Scott, Foresman, 1965)

Scriven, Michael, *Reasoning* (New York: McGraw-Hill, 1976)

Skyrms, Brian, *Choice and Chance* (Belmont, Cal.: Dickenson, 1966)

Snook, I. A., 'Teaching pupils to think, *Studies in Philosophy and Education*, vol. 8, no. 3 (Winter, 1974), pp. 154–5

Soltis, Jonas, 'Analysis and anomalies in philosophy of education', unpublished paper delivered at the Conference on New Directions in Philosophy of Education, held at the Ontario Institute for Studies in Education, Toronto, 1970

Soltis, Jonas, *An Introduction to the Analysis of Educational Concepts* (Reading, Mass.: Addison-Wesley, 1978)

Stewart, Bruce L., 'Testing for critical thinking: a review of the resources', in R. H. Ennis (ed.), *Rational Thinking Reports Number 2* (Urbana, Ill.: Bureau of Educational Research, 1979)

Sticht, Thomas G., 'The acquisition of literacy by children and adults', in F. B. Murray and J. J. Pikulsky (eds.), *The Acquisition of Reading* (Baltimore: University Park, 1978), pp. 131–62

Toulmin, Stephen, *The Uses of Argument* (Cambridge: Cambridge University Press, 1958)

Venesky, R. L., Calfee, R. C., and Chapman, R. S., 'Skills required for learning to read', in Doris V. Gunderson (ed.), *Language and Reading* (Washington, D.C.: University Park Press, 1970), pp. 36–54

Wason, P. C., and Johnson-Laird, P. N. (eds.), *Thinking and Reasoning* (Harmondsworth: Penguin, 1970)

Watson, Goodwin, and Glazer, Edward M., *Watson–Glazer Critical Thinking Appraisal* (New York: Test Department, Harcourt, Brace and World, 1964)

White, J. P., 'Creativity and education: a philosophical analysis', in Jane R. Martin (ed.), *Readings in the Philosophy of Education: A Study of Curriculum* (Boston: Allyn and Bacon, 1970), pp. 122–37

Wiener, M., and Cromer, W., 'Reading and reading difficulty: a conceptual analysis', *Harvard Education Review*, vol. 37, no. 4 (Fall, 1967), pp. 620–43

Wilson, Bryan R. (ed.), *Rationality* (New York: Harper & Row, 1970)

Wittgenstein, Ludwig, *Philosophical Investigations* (New York: Macmillan, 1973)

Woods, J. and Walton, J., 'On fallacies', *Journal of Critical Analysis*, vol. 4, no. 3 (October, 1972), pp. 103–12

Further Reading

Agassi, Joseph, 'Criteria for plausible arguments', *Mind*, vol. 83 (July, 1974), pp. 406–16

Annis, D., and Annis, Linda, 'Does philosophy improve critical thinking?', *Teaching Philosophy*, vol. 3, no. 2 (Fall, 1979)

Binkley, Robert, 'Theory of practical reasoning', *The Philosophical Review*, vol. 74 (October 1965), pp. 423–48

Black, Max, *Critical Thinking* (New York: Prentice-Hall, 1946)

Brody, Baruch A., *Logic: Theoretical and Applied* (Englewood Cliffs, N.J.: Prentice-Hall, 1973)

Copi, Irving M., *Introduction to Logic* (New York: Macmillan, 1953)

Cowan, J. L., 'The uses of argument ... an apology for logic', *Mind*, vol. 73 (January, 1964), pp. 27–45

Curtis, Charles K., 'Developing critical thinking skills in nonacademic social studies classes', *Alberta Journal of Educational Research*, vol. 26 (June, 1980), pp. 75–83

Flew, Antony, *Thinking Straight* (Buffalo, N.Y.: Prometheus Books, 1977)

Geach, Peter, *Reason and Argument* (Oxford: Basil Blackwell, 1976)

Geach, Peter, 'On teaching logic', *Philosophy*, vol. 54 (1979), pp. 5–17

Glymour, Clark, 'Relevant evidence', *Journal of Philosophy*, vol. 72 (August, 1975), pp. 405–26

Hassey, Gerald, 'Are there any good arguments that bad arguments are bad?', *Philosophy in Context*, vol. 4 (1975), pp. 61–77

Iseminger, Gary, 'Successful argument and rational belief', *Philosophy and Rhetoric*, vol. 7 (Winter, 1974), pp. 47–57

Lakin, R. D., 'Overhauling logic', *Midwest Quarterly*, vol. 6 (October, 1965) pp. 297–315

Salmon, Wesley, *Logic* (Englewood Cliffs, N.J.: Prentice-Hall, 1965)

Schouls, Peter A., 'Communication, argumentation and presupposition', *Philosophy and Rhetoric*, vol. 2 (1968), pp. 183–99

Weddle, Perry, *Argument: A Guide to Critical Thinking* (New York: McGraw-Hill, 1978)

Woods, John, and Walton, Douglas, 'Informal logic and critical thinking', *Education*, vol. 95 (Fall, 1974), pp. 84–6

Yalden-Thomson, D. C., 'Logic and informal logic', *Journal of Philosophy*, vol. 54 (May, 1957), pp. 141–2

Index